FOOTBALL ● SUPERSTARS

Walter Payton

FOOTBALL ⬤ SUPERSTARS

Tiki Barber

Tom Brady

John Elway

Brett Favre

Peyton Manning

Dan Marino

Donovan McNabb

Joe Montana

Walter Payton

Jerry Rice

Ben Roethlisberger

Barry Sanders

FOOTBALL ● SUPERSTARS

Walter Payton

Adam Woog

CHELSEA HOUSE
PUBLISHERS
An imprint of Infobase Publishing

WALTER PAYTON

Copyright © 2008 by Infobase Publishing

Chelsea House
An imprint of Infobase Publishing
132 West 31st Street
New York NY 10001

Library of Congress Cataloging-in-Publication Data
Woog, Adam, 1953-
  Walter Payton / Adam Woog.
    p. cm. -- (Football superstars)
  Includes bibliographical references and index.
  ISBN 978-0-7910-9567-6 (hardcover)
  1. Payton, Walter, 1954-1999. 2. Football players--United States--Biography--Juvenile
literature. I. Title. II. Series.

  GV939.P39W66 2008
  796.332092--dc22
  [B]

                    2007041030

Chelsea House books are available at special discounts when purchased in bulk quantities
for businesses, associations, institutions, or sales promotions. Please call our Special Sales
Department in New York at (212) 967-8800 or (800) 322-8755.

You can find Chelsea House on the World Wide Web at http://www.chelseahouse.com

Text design by Erik Lindstrom
Cover design by Ben Peterson

Printed in the United States of America

Bang EJB 10 9 8 7 6 5 4 3 2 1

This book is printed on acid-free paper.

All links and Web addresses were checked and verified to be correct at the time
of publication. Because of the dynamic nature of the Web, some addresses and links
may have changed since publication and may no longer be valid.

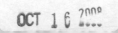

CONTENTS

1   Introducing Sweetness   7

2   A Boyhood in Columbia   16

3   College Life   28

4   Joining the Bears   39

5   Moving on Up   51

6   Seasons of Glory   64

7   Retiring Number 34   78

8   The End   89

9   Sweetness's Legacy   103

Statistics   114

Chronology   115

Timeline   116

Glossary   119

Bibliography   126

Further Reading   127

Picture Credits   128

Index   129

About the Author   135

Introducing Sweetness

Walter Payton got a late start in football, but he more than made up for lost time. Although he loved sports as a kid—all sports—he did not play on an organized football team until he was a junior in high school. After that, though, there was no stopping him. Walter went on to become one of the greatest players in **National Football League (NFL)** history. Many people will argue that he was *the* best, period.

Payton's nickname was "Sweetness," in part because he was usually friendly and cheerful in person and because he had a gentle, high-pitched voice. His college teammate Robert Brazile recalled, "The biggest thing I could remember about Walter was his smile. He also had a frown, but the thing that was behind that was a deep, loving, caring smile."

During his playing days, Walter Payton was known for his sunny disposition, which earned him the nickname "Sweetness." Here, Payton is all smiles as he prepares for a game against the Raiders at the Los Angeles Memorial Coliseum in December 1987.

"Sweetness" also was a good description of the elegant way Payton maneuvered around and through opposing players. But, in truth, Payton was hardly sweet when he was on a football field, facing a tough enemy. Many other words could describe him better—"tough," "quick," "agile," "smart," and "relentless" are a few.

Also, "fearless." Walter liked to hit his opponents as hard as they hit him, or harder. This was true even if they were bigger—*much* bigger. "Never die easy," was something his college coach had said, and Payton adopted it as his own motto. What he meant by it was that you should never give up too soon, never go down without a fight, and never take the easy way out—at least on the field.

As a result, Payton was brilliant at his main job, carrying the ball down the field as a **running back**. But he also was a superb all-around athlete, able to fill other roles as needed. He was nearly as skilled at passing and receiving as he was at running and **blocking**. During his college career, Payton's coach used him occasionally as a kicker, and as a professional he even played **quarterback** during a game in 1984, when the starting quarterback and **backup** were injured. At 5'10" and about 200 pounds, Payton was hardly the biggest player on the field; he was simply better than the others. Mike Ditka, his longtime coach with the Chicago Bears and himself a legend in the sports world, commented, "Pound for pound as a football player, Walter [was] the best I've ever seen."

WITH "DA BEARS"

This amazing athlete spent his entire professional career, 13 seasons, with the Chicago Bears. (Prior to that, he had been a star on his high school team—earning all-state honors after his senior season—and then enjoyed a record-setting college career.) For most of his years in the NFL, though, Payton was a diamond in the rough—a brilliant player on a not-so-brilliant team.

His career with "Da Bears" (as Chicago fans call the team) fell into three distinct periods. The year Payton joined the team, 1975, also marked the beginning of Jack Pardee's three-year stint as the Bears' head coach. It was not a satisfying time. Under Pardee, the team had a sub-.500 record (though they did make the playoffs in his final season). The Bears were rough and tough but unfocused, and Payton was by far the team's best player.

The team got a little better in 1978, when Neill Armstrong replaced Pardee as head coach, and really improved when Mike

MOTTOES TO LIVE BY

"Never die easy," was one of Jackson State football coach Bob Hill's mottoes. He meant that nobody should ever give up easily—you should always fight until the end. Walter Payton adopted the phrase as his own words to live by, even using them as the title of his best-selling autobiography. He remarked in that book that the words meant, "Don't let them just take you down. Punish them and make them pay. So that next time you come at them it will make them cringe." During his days at Jackson State and later with the Chicago Bears, Payton rarely ran out of bounds or avoided a hit. He was the consummate professional; giving his all on every single play. After his football career had come to an end, he continued to give his heart and soul to every endeavor he was involved with, including the charitable organization he cofounded with his wife, the Walter and Connie Payton Foundation. As Payton once said after a disappointing loss that ended the 1984 Bears season: "Tomorrow is promised to no one." He truly lived by these mantras each and every day of his life.

Ditka became head coach in 1982. During these years, the late 1970s into the mid-1980s, the Bears began to form into a championship team. A number of other talented players were added, and the team became clearly focused. Slowly but steadily, Da Bears developed into one of the top teams in the NFL.

TOILING FOR THE BEARS

The only constant on the field during the late 1970s and early 1980s was Walter Payton, and he more or less carried the team through its long period of mediocrity. Despite the fact that he was one of the better players in the league, however, Sweetness managed to avoid the trap many sports stars fall into: developing an inflated ego.

He remained a straightforward guy who remembered where he came from, never treated people with contempt, and tried to find a common ground with others. In this (and many other aspects of his personality), he was the opposite of what people have come to expect from sports celebrities. Longtime NFL commissioner Paul Tagliabue commented, "He was in many ways what we don't expect a superstar to be: open, accessible, genuine, down to earth, a unifier, and a binder."

During his years with the Bears, Payton reached a number of important personal milestones. For instance, he became the youngest player in league history to be named NFL MVP when he earned the honor in 1977 at the age of 23. He also bested the career rushing record that legendary Cleveland Browns running back Jim Brown had held for two decades. And he accomplished the crowning achievement of any NFL player's career: leading his team to victory in the Super Bowl.

PAYTON LEFT, PAYTON RIGHT . . .

Walter Payton retired after the 1987 season, ending his professional career at the age of 33. For 13 years, he had helped lead the Bears to prominence and was the team's best player—so much so, in fact, that the standard joke was: What's Chicago's game plan? Payton left, Payton right, Payton middle, **punt**.

To many of Da Fans (as Chicago sports fans are known), not even the six National Basketball Association (NBA) titles the Chicago Bulls racked up could surpass Payton's achievements. He was not only a nice guy; he also was a record-breaking athlete. The numbers tell the story:

- 16,726 career rushing **yards**
- 3,838 carries
- 110 **touchdowns**
- 275 rushing yards in a single game
- 10 thousand-yard rushing seasons
- 5 fifteen-hundred-yard rushing seasons
- 77 hundred-yard rushing games
- 2 NFL MVP awards
- 5 straight **National Football Conference (NFC)** rushing titles (1976 to 1980)
- 9 Pro Bowl games
- 1 Super Bowl victory

A MUTUAL LOVE AFFAIR

As he was racking up these extraordinary accomplishments during the first part of his career, Payton never complained, at least publicly, about the fact that the rest of his team was only mediocre. He never pouted, and he never expressed a desire to be traded. The Bears were usually an average team—fans sometimes called them "the Sleeping Bears"—but he liked playing for them, liked living in Chicago, and liked the people he met there. "It was just home to me," he remarked, "and I wasn't about to make a home elsewhere."

Payton was especially appreciative of Da Fans. Chicago residents are known for having a strong work ethic, and that was something he could relate to. He also knew that without the fans he would not have had a career, and he was grateful for their support. In turn, Da Fans loved Payton. He was a beloved celebrity, Chicago's biggest athletic star in the years between the retirement of Cubs Hall of Famer Ernie Banks in 1971 and the rise in the mid-1980s of one of the greatest players in NBA history, Bulls forward Michael Jordan.

Chicago fans loved Payton for several reasons. The city is renowned as a tough-minded town, and Da Fans appreciated Payton's ruggedness. Even when he was hurt, Payton missed only one game during four years of college and 13 years in the NFL. (The one game he missed during this astonishing streak came in his rookie year with the Bears, when Coach Pardee refused to let him play due to an injured ankle.) Da Fans also loved Payton's no-nonsense, get-it-done attitude: just get in there and do the job, no matter what it takes and no matter who gets the glory. Payton was far from being a demanding, self-centered prima donna.

"THAT COMBINATION IS A TREASURE"

Da Fans also loved Payton because he always had time for them. He was amiable with everyone he met, always ready with a kind word or a joke. And he was always willing to sign autographs or spend a moment chatting with a fan.

But there was more to Walter Payton than just an easygoing, friendly jock. He was a complex man with many, often contradictory, sides. He could be shy and reserved, especially around reporters—he hated talking to the press. And there were moments of depression and sadness in his life, as there are in any person's life. Furthermore, Payton remained a private person; he had countless acquaintances but only a few close friends, and even his beloved family often found him enigmatic.

In addition, Payton was always hard on himself. This was never more true than with his training regimen. Beginning in high school and continuing through college and his professional career, Payton designed a workout program that was incredibly difficult. Year after year, he worked so hard in the

Chicago Bears supporters were not the only ones who appreciated Walter Payton's tough style of play and willingness to acknowledge the fans. Here, Payton high-fives fans as he enters Lambeau Field for a game against the Bears' archrival, the Green Bay Packers.

off-season that training camp felt like a vacation to him. He often invited others to join him, but few could keep up with him. Coach Ditka recalled, "His regimen was much harder than any NFL strength coach's regimen. He had a regimen that defied what the U.S. Marines were doing."

This tough, no-nonsense attitude toward his training was in sharp contrast to other aspects of his personality, such as his sense of humor. Throughout his life, Payton loved to laugh, and he especially loved practical jokes. He frequently used humor to bring people together or to defuse a tense situation, saying, "The one thing I have always found about different races is everyone likes to laugh. It is universal. Comedy can really bring people together, so that is what I tried to do."

And though he was serious about football, Payton was often playful on the field. For instance, he sometimes mischievously unlaced the shoes of referees as he lay on the ground after a **tackle**. Another football great, former Oakland Raiders head coach and now NFL analyst John Madden, remarked, "I thought Walter Payton was the greatest football player who ever lived. He did it . . . better than anyone. And he had more fun. [T]hat combination is a treasure."

RETIREMENT

Payton made a great living playing football—at one point, he was the highest-paid player in the NFL (although the money pales in comparison to today's megasalaries). For the most part, Payton invested his money wisely. In retirement, therefore, he was well off financially. He could have done little else but relax and spend time with his family: his wife, Connie, who had been his college sweetheart, and their children, Jarrett and Brittney.

But Payton was restless and energetic. At first, therefore, retirement was difficult for him; football had been his life, and, as with many people who love their jobs, the transition from work to retirement was not easy. Soon, however, he found ways to keep busy. He had a variety of business projects, including a protracted but unsuccessful attempt to become the first African-American owner of an NFL team. He also devoted himself to charitable causes.

Then, only a decade or so into retirement, life took an unexpected turn. This immensely strong and vital man, who for years had played the roughest of sports, became ill. He had developed a rare and fatal liver disease.

In the last, painful year of his life, Walter Payton taught the world about courage—about facing a terrible disease with dignity and inner strength. When he died in 1999, countless fans and friends mourned a remarkable man, one whose story began in a small town in southern Mississippi.

A Boyhood in Columbia

Walter Jerry Payton was born on July 25, 1954, in Columbia, Mississippi. His parents were Peter and Alyne Payton. (Some sources list Peter's name as Edward.) After the other Payton kids, Eddie and Pam, Walter was the youngest in the family.

Columbia, the seat of Marion County in south-central Mississippi, was then a small town of about 7,000 residents. Life there moved slowly, the people were easygoing, and the community was tightly knit. The Paytons knew everyone in their neighborhood, Smith Quarter. Church and school were important to the Paytons, and to everyone they knew.

But it was not an ideal life. Columbia was subject to the same strict racial segregation that existed throughout the American South. And, like many rural towns in the South, Columbia was economically poor. The Paytons, like everyone they knew, never had much money. This was good in some ways, Walter later remarked; it helped him understand that wealth was not the most important thing in life. "When everybody has nothing," he remarked, "it's not as big a deal."

HARD WORK

Walter's parents worked at the main business in Columbia, a parachute company called Pioneer Recovery Systems. They worked different shifts, so that someone was always home for the kids. The family kept two gardens: a small vegetable patch next to their house on Hendrick Street and a five-acre plot outside town. Walter's father also sometimes did odd jobs to earn extra money, such as hauling items in his truck.

Walter's parents worked long and hard. Their strong work ethic was a powerful influence on Walter, Pam, and Eddie. The children learned the importance of doing everything to the best of their abilities, whether it was work or play.

Education also was important to the Payton family, so the kids' studies came first. When they finished, they had regular chores, such as helping out in their parents' gardens. And if Alyne saw that her children were idle, she always found something for them to do. Walter sometimes hid in the outhouse just to avoid extra chores!

THE TOPSOIL

One chore in particular made a lasting impression on Walter. Every summer, his mother bought a load of topsoil and gave her boys the task of spreading it around their yard. This was messy, hard, and time-consuming work—especially because Walter and Eddie had just one wheelbarrow and one shovel between them. Adding to the difficulty was the fact that Mississippi's summer rains often turned the dirt to mud.

Walter hated this work. He was delighted to have a chance to quit. He recalled, "I was never so happy as when [I] started

When the Payton kids—Walter, Pam, and Eddie—were growing up, their parents, Alyne and Peter, instilled a solid work ethic in them. Thanks to Walter's desire to be the best, he was able to succeed on the football field. Alyne and Eddie Payton are pictured here in 2006 talking to former New York congressman Jack Kemp (left) and Mississippi governor Haley Barbour at a news conference for USA Football, a nonprofit organization that promotes youth and amateur football.

Little League baseball when I was 10. That got me from hauling all that dirt."

Years later, Walter realized that it had all been a trick. His mother did not need the topsoil; she got it just to keep the boys occupied during the summer. Still, the chore had a positive effect. Walter said later that moving all that dirt around helped develop his muscles early in life. It also taught him to overcome tough obstacles.

EXPLORING

Of course, not all of Walter's time was spent at school or doing chores. Whenever they could, he and his siblings played—

usually outside, and all day if possible. Walter liked to fish and swim in the nearby Pearl River and to camp in the woods. He also loved to play games and sports, either with his friends or on his own. He once remarked, "As soon as breakfast was done, we'd be out the door." When his friends were not around to join him, Walter made up elaborate one-kid games patterned after characters he saw while watching television. He recalled,

> I ran and jumped and played in the woods, pretending I was Robin Hood or some other hero I had seen on television. I might be Sir Lancelot or Zorro. It never occurred to me that these heroes were white. I didn't care. To me, they were good guys instead of bad. They were brave and strong. That's what I wanted to be. A good guy.

No matter what he did, he did it with intensity. Although Walter was relatively small, his family, friends, and neighbors remember him as having boundless energy. They also say that he was cheerful and full of jokes and mischief. He later admitted to some of the tricks he and Eddie used to play on Pam, such as putting a bucket of water above a door so that it fell on her head when she opened it.

Walter especially liked exploring distant corners of Columbia and the surrounding countryside with Eddie and his other friends. The adventurous boys thought nothing of jumping onto moving trains or river barges, exploring the woods, or playing in the factory where Walter's parents worked. Such spots were, as Walter once remarked, "perfect places for getting into trouble."

GAMES

Later, Walter would become famous for his ability to outmaneuver his opponents. His gift for slipping past defenders seemed almost magical. As Walter often pointed out, this distinctive, bob-and-weave style had its origins in the childhood games he played.

For example, when he was a kid, he invented a game called "war." In it, he played both sides, spinning and jumping away from imaginary enemies. Because he was both the good guy and the bad guy, Walter naturally started thinking about the strategies his opponents would use—and how he should react to them.

Another aspect of the games Walter played during his childhood would also become important when he grew up. As a professional football player, Walter's style was not to avoid defensive players. Instead of running out of bounds to avoid an opponent, he ran straight at them and tried to maneuver around them—or to hit them just as hard as they hit him. This habit started when he was a boy.

It came about because there never seemed to be enough players to field an entire team. So Walter and his friends scaled the game down, playing on only a small portion of the high school field. This gave them very little room for maneuvering around each other. As a result, Walter learned to face the defense head-on, jumping over or dancing around them—or hitting them straight on.

HIGH SCHOOL BALL

When Walter started high school, he first attended Jefferson High, just a short distance from his home. His brother, Eddie, three years older, was a senior and a star football player there. But Walter did not go out for football as a freshman. He chose to play drums in the school marching band instead. But when he became a junior, Walter decided that he would try out for the football team. He joked that he switched when he realized that girls liked boys in football uniforms better than boys in band uniforms. But he also did not want to compete with

Eddie. Walter's friend and teammate Edward "Sugar Man" Moses recalled that Walter "was always quiet and reserved, sort of living . . . behind an older brother who [was] famous."

As a freshman, Walter would have been on the field with Eddie. But by Walter's junior year, Eddie had gone on to college. He had earned a football scholarship to Jackson State University, in Jackson, Mississippi. As a result, Walter decided he would play football. He quickly asserted himself as an agile running back, and by the end of his first season he was, like his brother, a star.

SCHOOL INTEGRATION

The next year, when Walter was a junior, he and his classmates were affected by an important shift in American society. This was a landmark change in education: the full integration of public schools.

For many decades, public schools in the South had been segregated by race. This separation was part of the South's strict (if often unspoken) policy of racial segregation in general. In Columbia and elsewhere in the region, blacks and whites interacted in some ways—and in others remained quite separate.

One clear aspect of this division was in education. Walter, like the other African-American kids in town, had always attended all-black schools. Like other black schools in the South, Walter's schools were supposed to be "separate but equal," but in reality had far worse facilities and poorer materials than the schools attended by whites.

However, the times were changing. The civil rights movement, the fight for equal rights for black citizens, had been creating change during the past couple of decades. One major change came in 1954, when the U.S. Supreme Court handed down a landmark decision: that segregation in public schools was unconstitutional. With this ruling, *Brown v. Board of Education*, America's schools were forced to integrate.

"JUST A NEW THING"

This change came slowly in places such as southern Mississippi. Not until early 1970, midway through Walter's junior year, did Jefferson High School merge with the local white high school, Columbia. By this time, most of the ugly and violent incidents that had occurred during the first few years of integration were no longer a threat.

In fact, it was quite a smooth transition for Walter. One of Walter's new classmates and teammates, Forrest Dantin, recalled, "The only thing that happened the first day was when five guys stood outside for about an hour or two and protested, and they weren't even students of Columbia High at that time."

To Walter and most of his classmates, the merger of Jefferson and Columbia was not a very big deal—it was just an interesting new aspect of their lives. He recalled, "Growing up we just accepted that blacks and whites attended separate schools. It was just the way it was. . . . It wasn't really something you thought about as a kid. So when we heard that they were going to integrate the high schools it wasn't a big social victory, just a new thing."

GOOD NEWS FOR THE TEAM

School integration had an immediate and positive effect on Walter's football prospects. Columbia High School had better facilities and equipment, but Jefferson High School had more talent. When the two joined, they became not only the first integrated team in the town's history—they were stronger than either had been separately.

It was not always easy. At first, there were occasional confrontations as the two groups got to know each other. Ignorance or nervousness caused a few unpleasant incidents. Walter, already a joker, used humor to break the tension. He understood that laughter is common to all people. His teammate Ricky Joe Graves recalled that Walter "loved to lighten things up in what could have been a tense locker room."

Even so, Walter did experience some difficulties in his first year as a Columbia player. For one thing, he was not used to the superior equipment and facilities available at Columbia; the version of football he knew was much less sophisticated than what was now expected of him. He recalled, "I had never worn the pads and all that stuff, and I didn't know the first things about real fundamentals."

Furthermore, he made a few dumb mistakes. During his first practice, for instance, he scored a touchdown—but in the wrong **end zone**! Walter was so scared of his bigger teammates that he panicked and simply ran into the nearest end zone he could find.

"SOMETHING REAL SPECIAL"

He overcame these mistakes, however, and quickly emerged as the team's star. He was strong and speedy. He conquered his fear of oncoming opponents. And he had wonderful control, thanks in part to a terrific sense of balance. Walter had such a great sense of balance that he could walk long distances on his hands. And not just that—he could turn corners and go up stairs while walking on them! Apparently, Walter's strength and size ran in his family. One of his teammates on the Columbia High School football squad, Quin Breland, told this story:

> One summer I was working at a warehouse, where the cotton gin was. I was in there loading some stuff . . . and I saw this older black man walking by with a two-wheeled buggy with a bale of cotton on it, and those things were heavy. As he walked by, I could see he had a tight-fitting T-shirt on and that he was built like Schwarzenegger. I figured I had to see what the deal was, so I spoke to him, told him who I was, and he told me who he was. He said his name was Payton, and I asked him if he was any kin to Walter, and he said, "Walter's my nephew." This guy was at least sixty

years old, but I swear he looked like he could be playing professional football right then. He was ready to rip out of that T-shirt.

Walter's inherited athletic prowess made him a one-man show. Breland also recalled, "You didn't have to do much; just **snap** the ball, and it would be handed off to Walter, and then you could just stand around and watch him run." Everyone else also could see that they were in the presence of an extraordinary player. Charles Boston was Walter's coach at Jefferson and assistant coach at Columbia after the schools merged. He recalled that, even then, he could tell Walter had a bright future: "I'm not saying I knew back then he was going to be as great as he turned out, but I knew he was going to be something real special, and I'd been right before."

TRAINING AND SCORING

Boston and head coach Tommy Davis worked the Columbia team hard. Walter took his own training regimen a step further, however. The strenuous exercise program he created for himself became legendary.

Walter jogged to and from practice every day from home, more than a mile each way. He also regularly ran through the woods, darting around trees as if they were defenders. And he wore old army boots while he ran, so that when he put his cleats on they seemed light by comparison.

Furthermore, with his older brother Eddie's guidance, Walter began lifting weights. This was unusual; it was years before weight training became standard practice for high school athletes. Teammate Edward Moses recalled, "When the rest of us were getting high school-type training, he was getting college-type training. And he was keeping it to himself. He got really big and strong."

Walter played several memorable games as a member of the Columbia Wildcats. In one contest, Columbia was losing,

6-0, in the first half against its rival, Prentiss High School from Prentiss, Mississippi. But Walter got the ball and ran 95 yards for a touchdown. Then he scored again, this time from 65 yards out, giving Columbia a 14-6 victory.

OTHER PURSUITS

Of course, Walter also had a life beyond football, which was helped by his generally sunny personality. He was reserved, especially with people he did not know well, but he also was optimistic and even-tempered. His girlfriend at the time, Jill Brewer, recalled, "He was a very nice, sweet guy, kind of shy. . . . He was just a fun-loving person." His teacher L. E. Daniels, who had Walter as a student at both Jefferson and Columbia, commented, "He had a great personality, and I never saw him angry."

Walter did well academically, getting above-average grades. He was active in several school organizations, including choir and the science and French clubs. And he played baseball, basketball, and track.

For the track team, Walter normally competed in the sprints, but at one meet he took the place of an injured long jumper. Walter had never even tried that event, but the coach gave him a quick lesson. Not only did he win the event—he set a new record and went on to become the state champion!

ON TO COLLEGE

Nonetheless, it was on the football field that he shone the brightest. After leading Columbia to an 8–2 record his senior season, Payton was named to the all-state team, and it was clear that he had a future as a college athlete. But in 1971, the year he graduated, there were not many scholarship opportunities for African-American athletes, even outstanding ones.

Few of the big powerhouse schools were interested in recruiting black players. They typically ignored them in favor of white players. Change was coming, but only slowly. Legendary

Despite his impressive play on the football field, Walter Payton was not recruited by many top-ranked colleges coming out of high school. He eventually wound up at Jackson State University, where he joined his brother, Eddie, in the backfield. Payton is pictured here on the campus of Jackson State, showing off his trademark high-step style of running.

University of Alabama coach Paul "Bear" Bryant summed up the feelings of many college coaches when he remarked, "I won't be the first to let in black players . . . but I won't be the last."

Only three schools offered Payton a scholarship. Not even the University of Southern Mississippi in Hattiesburg, which was only 30 miles from Columbia, was interested. Of the schools that did offer scholarships, only the University of Kansas was nationally ranked. The others, Jackson State University and Alcorn State University, were smaller, traditionally black colleges in Mississippi.

Payton accepted Kansas's offer and attended the school briefly, but it was too far from home and he was unhappy there. Also, his mother was eager to have him closer; she urged him to attend Jackson State, so he returned to Mississippi and enrolled there. Payton's life as a college football player was about to begin.

College Life

By the time he started at Jackson State, Walter Payton had overcome his reluctance to play alongside his older brother. Now he enjoyed playing on the same team as Eddie, who also played running back. The backfield they shared was called "Payton's Place"; this was a joking reference to a famous 1950s novel by Grace Metalious, *Peyton Place*. (After a stint as a teacher and football coach in Memphis, Tennessee, Eddie would go on to his own career in the NFL. From 1977 to 1982, he played for the Cleveland Browns, Detroit Lions, Kansas City Chiefs, and Minnesota Vikings.)

Walter enjoyed being part of the Jackson State Tigers. His easygoing nature fit in well with the casual attitude at a smaller school. Looking back on it, he felt that Jackson State may have been less prestigious than the powerhouse colleges he might

During the one year they spent together playing for Jackson State, Eddie and Walter Payton combined to form an outstanding one-two punch in the backfield. As a result, fans dubbed the running back tandem "Payton's Place," a reference to the 1950s novel *Peyton Place*. Here, Walter (right) and Eddie, who played five years in the NFL, walk off the field after an exhibition game between the Cleveland Browns and Chicago Bears in 1977.

have attended, but it also was far less stressful. He liked the relative lack of pressure it created for him.

He also appreciated the small number of problems on the field and elsewhere that could have been caused by inflated egos. Because Jackson State was not prominent nationally, Payton's teammates were not celebrities with oversized opinions of themselves. The Tigers' coach, Bob Hill, nurtured this down-to-earth attitude among his players. Payton recalled, "Coach Hill just wanted me to stay planted and not really get suckered into [celebrity] because once you do, that's it. Once you get soft, once you take success and let it go to your head, you are done."

A SOLID GROUNDING

Coach Hill was a tough, no-nonsense leader. He firmly believed that each of his players should be a complete and well-rounded performer on the field. He therefore helped Payton perfect his knowledge of the basics of football by playing him in several **positions** at various times. As a result, Payton got at least a little experience with almost every aspect of the game.

Still, Payton's strong suits remained blocking and running, and Coach Hill helped him refine these skills. For example, Hill worked with Payton to perfect his simple but solid approach to running. This was a style in which Payton kept his shoulders down and stepped high with his knees, smashing right into and through defensive players instead of trying to avoid them.

Hill also worked his players hard. His practice sessions were legendary; some members of the Jackson State team swore that their practices were tougher than any game they played. Robert Brazile, Payton's teammate and another future NFL player, commented, "I think I was ready for professional football by my sophomore year or junior year because of what we had endured under Coach Hill, with all the workouts we had. If somebody else was doing twenty of something, we'd do sixty; if they did sixty, we did 120. We were workaholics."

PRIVATE WORKOUTS

Payton did not simply endure these backbreaking practices. He endured them and then asked for more. In fact, he did not even take a vacation from working out during the off-season. He wanted to stay in shape year-round, so he designed punishing workouts to do on his own.

These workouts frequently took place on two riverside pieces of land near the Jackson State campus. One was a steep sandbank where Payton paced off a 65-yard course. Running on this sandbank was fiendishly hard to do. Because of the loose sand and the bank's steepness, Payton's 65-yard course was equivalent to about one and a half football fields. The other spot was a short, steep rise he called the levee. At 45 degrees, it was even steeper than the sandbank.

Payton did not let himself slack off when it came to his riverside workouts. Not even the sweltering heat of a Mississippi summer kept him from his routines. A typical daily workout for Payton was 10 times up and down the sandbank, 20 up and down the levee, then an hour of running up and down the steps of the university's stadium. Sometimes other players would join him for these routines, but never for very long. No one could keep up with him.

MEETING CONNIE

Coach Hill kept a close eye on the workouts his players engaged in, as well as other aspects of their game, but his influence on his players extended far beyond football. He liked to keep tabs on their private lives, because he wanted to make sure they behaved correctly and honorably. The coach could be intimidating in this regard, Payton recalled: "We were afraid to get in trouble. He probably would have taken you out and spanked your butt just like a parent would do."

On at least one occasion, this ongoing effort to give direction to his players' lives involved romance—and had a permanent impact on that player's life. This happened when

Coach Hill introduced Walter Payton to the woman who would become his wife: Connie Norwood.

As they later realized, Connie had seen Walter on television even before they met in person. Payton was a good dancer, and he and a partner had recently won a contest on a local television dance show, *24 Karat Black Gold*. The prize was a trip to Los Angeles for an appearance on the nationally broadcast dance show *Soul Train*.

Connie first saw Walter when that episode of *Soul Train* aired. He was garbed in seventies-style clothing for the occasion: bell-bottoms, platform shoes, and an open shirt showing off his toned body. Of course, Connie did not know then that she was catching a glimpse of her future husband.

DATING CONNIE

In fact, Connie did not meet Walter in person until Coach Hill arranged it. Hill knew Connie because he was dating her aunt. Connie, two years younger than Walter, was still in high school in New Orleans at the time.

Hill liked Connie. The coach thought she was a levelheaded young woman, someone who could help his star running back stay focused on academics and athletics. He arranged for the two to meet, but there was little mutual attraction at first. Connie thought Walter was nice but too shy. For his part, Payton was not in a romantic mood at all—he spent the evening talking about another girl. He told Connie that he liked this girl, but that her parents disliked him.

After that first meeting, nothing else special happened between the two teens for several months, although they talked occasionally on the phone. Then, later in the school year, Payton asked if he could come and visit her in New Orleans. She agreed. However, he was shy and nervous around her family—so nervous, in fact, that he ate no dinner, which annoyed Connie's mother. Later that evening, Walter admitted to Connie that he was starving, and he asked if he could have a bowl of cereal or something.

Connie had planned to go to college in New Orleans, her hometown. But Coach Hill convinced her to apply to Jackson State and try out for the Jaycettes, the school's dance team. She

DANCING ON AND OFF THE FIELD

Long before the popular reality television series *Dancing with the Stars* aired on ABC, Walter Payton was making a name for himself on another popular television dance show. Although former Dallas Cowboys running back Emmitt Smith, the same player who broke Payton's NFL career rushing record, has staked his claim as football's best dancer by winning the *Dancing with the Stars'* Season 3 title with professional dancer Cheryl Burke, Smith would have a hard time outdoing Payton on the dance floor. While at Jackson State, Payton excelled on the football field, but he also loved to dance, and he was well known on campus as a great dancer. During his freshman year, he had the opportunity to appear on *Soul Train*, a nationally syndicated television program that has been on the air since 1971. Dancers move to the beat of R&B, soul, and, more recently, hip-hop music. Perhaps the first notice in the news media of Payton's abilities on the gridiron and dance floor came on October 11, 1973, when the Jackson (Mississippi) *Clarion-Ledger* published the following note:

> Walter Payton, Jackson State halfback who the Tigers refer to as their Heisman Trophy candidate, just can't stop dancing, either on or off the field. On the field, the five foot eleven [*sic*], two hundred pounder danced his way to nearly a thousand yards rushing and receiving last year and scored seventeen points, and he threatens to top those figures as he has over six hundred yards rushing and sixty points in five games this season.

was accepted to the school and became part of the dance team. When she started there as a freshman, Payton was a junior. They began to see more and more of each other, and by the end of the school year they were dating regularly.

"AN ALL-AROUND GOOD GUY"

In addition to his commitment to football and his developing relationship with Connie, Walter kept busy at Jackson State in other ways. For one thing, he was pursuing a degree in communications. He had little time for anything but his studies, his girlfriend, and athletics; his reputation was hardly that of a partier. Teammate Douglas Baker recalled, "He was an all-around good guy, a clean-cut guy. He didn't do any drugs and drank so little that if he had a half-can of beer, he'd be high as a kite, and we'd be laughing at him." Focusing on football, Connie, and academics kept Payton grounded. Inflated egos have been—and still are—treacherous roadblocks for many gifted athletes. If star players are given too much attention, privileges, and special treatment, they can become conceited and lose sight of their true goals. Rodney Phillips, Payton's teammate and roommate at Jackson State, commented that Walter stayed on the straight and narrow despite his obvious talent:

> Walter got past that. Walter . . . believed in fundamentals, he believed in hard work, and then he had the talent to go along with it. There were people who were faster, there were people who were quicker, there were people who were stronger, but there was nobody who was all of those.

Still, he occasionally found time to hang out with his friends. With them, he had a reputation as a high-spirited guy who loved to clown around. Another teammate, Vernon Perry, recalled, "Walter was the kind of guy who liked to have fun. He wasn't a dull person. He might walk up to you and bite you in the shoulder or come up behind you and just holler real loud. He would always do some kind of prank or joke to get your attention."

But Payton also had a different side to his personality. As he had always been, he was reserved around people he did not know. Sometimes, he also was moody and thoughtful even among friends. Rodney Phillips said, "Walter was more complex than he let on. He had a lot of serious moods. When something upset him he got a little quiet or a little sullen. He was very concerned about what people thought."

A STANDOUT PLAYER

Throughout his four years at Jackson State, Payton was an outstanding football player, just as he had been in high school. His focus, ambition, and talent—and those awesome workouts—assured his success. Douglas Baker recalled, "We knew he was going to be a great player from the first day. The first look we got of him in pads in practice we knew that."

Payton was not just a superb athlete; he also was a reliable one. His belief in hard work and the importance of toughing things out, playing even through the worst pain, paid off. As a result, he did not miss even a single game during his college career.

This commitment to playing every game was an important point of pride with Payton. On one occasion, for example, his ankle was hurting quite a bit, and by any normal standards he should not have played in the game. No one would have blamed him for sitting out. But he insisted that the team's trainers tape his ankle tightly so that he could play through the pain—and he scored a couple of touchdowns on that bum ankle.

Payton was not just the best player at Jackson State. He was the best in the entire SWAC (Southwestern Athletic Conference). And he faced some extremely tough competition to reach that level. Just on Payton's team alone, there were some amazing players. Twenty of the Tigers who played with him during his college career would, in time, also become NFL players.

AN OUTSTANDING COLLEGE CAREER

If not for the fact that Jackson State was a small, mostly over-looked school, Payton would probably have been generally acknowledged as the top college player in the country. The numbers speak for themselves. First, there was the team's record: During 1971 through 1974, the period Payton was there, Jackson State's record was 33–11–1.

And, of course, there was Payton's outstanding individual statistics. He set nine school records. He rushed for 3,563 career yards, with an average of 6.1 yards per carry. He scored a record 66 touchdowns. And he was a two-time Little All-American.

The impressive numbers went on and on. Payton once scored 46 points in a single game. He led the nation's college players in scoring in 1973 with 160 points. And his 464 career points (66 touchdowns, five **field goals**, and 53 **extra points**) set a **National Collegiate Athletic Association (NCAA)** record.

But even these statistics were not enough to get him the national attention he deserved. That was because schools such as Jackson State did not receive much publicity. This fact was made clear when Payton was a senior and finished well behind the leaders in the Heisman Trophy voting. He undoubtedly would have finished higher in the voting if he had gone to a larger, more visible and prestigious university.

Publicly, Payton tried to make it seem that winning the Heisman Trophy was not a big deal. In private, however, he was disappointed, and sometimes he found it difficult to hold back his emotions. When a reporter compared him to his Heisman rivals, Ohio State running back Archie Griffin and University of Southern California running back Anthony Davis, Payton snapped, "No comparison. I'm better than they are, and I know it."

Although Walter Payton was snubbed by Heisman Trophy voters, he did win a number of awards while playing for Jackson State. In addition to twice being named a Little All-American, he was named the Black College offensive player of the year in 1974. Payton (left) is pictured here with Alcorn State's Marino Casem (center), the coach of the year, and Grambling State's Gary Johnson, the defensive player of the year, at the second annual Black College All-American Football Team Awards banquet in New York City in December 1974.

HEADING TO THE NFL

Many observers felt that Payton had a right to be bitter about the Heisman snub. Probably, they pointed out, the result would have been different if he had attended a larger school. Nonetheless, Payton often said later in life that he did not regret missing out on attending a powerhouse school. He felt that what he gained at the smaller school was worth the trade-off.

Specifically, he felt that the warmth and friendship he found at Jackson State were too important to have given up. And he felt that he received an excellent education, both on and off the field. He later remarked, "I tell you what I gained at Jackson State in terms of knowledge, in terms of being able to socialize and the education I got—I wouldn't trade it for all the Heisman Trophies in the world."

And, though he did not win the trophy, Payton was highly regarded by NFL teams, even if the general public did not know about him. He was definitely on the national map, and the professional football scouts who keep tabs on promising players were certainly aware of him. Payton graduated late in 1974, half a year early, having completed his bachelor's degree in communications. But he was clearly pointed toward a career in football, and—with good reason—he had high hopes. At the age of 20, Payton was poised to enter the world of the NFL.

Joining the Bears

The 1975 NFL draft went very well for Walter Payton. Several teams showed interest in drafting him, notably the Dallas Cowboys. However, it was the Chicago Bears that got Payton, choosing him in the first round.

He was the first running back selected that year and the fourth player picked overall. The only players chosen before him were quarterback Steve Bartkowski (who went to the Atlanta Falcons), **defensive tackle** Randy White (who went to the Cowboys), and **guard** Ken Huff (who went to the Baltimore Colts).

Payton was delighted at the outcome of the draft. He was going to the pros! To celebrate, he and some friends rented some motorcycles and took off for a day of joyriding.

Soon after, Payton signed a three-year contract with the Bears. Counting incentives, the contract paid him nearly half a million dollars, plus a $126,000 signing bonus. This may seem low by today's standards, but it was excellent pay for the time—above-average money for a rookie in the NFL in those days. And unlike many of today's football players, Payton did not have any plans to hold out and demand as much money as possible. Bill Tobin, who scouted Payton while the running back was at Jackson State and later served as the Bears' executive in charge of personnel, has compared Payton's attitude toward contract negotiations with that of today's NFL players. He noted that some current players like to hold off on signing their contracts to gain advantages:

> You know, they're drafted No. 1 and they sign two games after the season starts. That's nothing more than absolute selfishness, and Walter didn't have an ounce of that in his body. . . .
>
> What may be his greatest tribute is that he signed a three-year contract to begin his career. Then he signed another three-year contract, and after he finished that he signed another three-year contract, and after he finished that he signed another three-year contract, and after he finished that he signed a one-year contract.
>
> He played thirteen years and never held out of training camp one day. Never. He honored every sentence, every paragraph of his contract.

TAKING A CHANCE

The Chicago Bears chose Payton, of course, because they needed him. Specifically, they needed a great running back. The Bears had a long tradition of excellent running backs, most recently Gale Sayers, the legendary star from the University of Kansas. But Sayers had retired in 1971, and the team's executives were looking for someone to fill the void he had left.

Not everyone in the Bears organization was convinced that Payton was the best choice. But previous first-round draft

Before Walter Payton arrived in Chicago in 1975, Gale Sayers was the best running back in Bears franchise history. Despite an injury-plagued career, Sayers rushed for nearly 5,000 yards, scored 48 touchdowns, and was a four-time Pro Bowl player for the Bears during a career that spanned seven seasons.

picks for the Bears had come from small schools, as did Payton, and those players had done well. So the team's new coach, Jack Pardee, and its general manager, Jim Finks, decided to take a chance on Payton.

The Bears chose Payton for another reason besides the fact that they needed a good running back. More broadly, the team simply needed some new talent. The Bears had been suffering through a long, humiliating series of losing seasons. The coach preceding Pardee, Abe Gibron, had racked up a dismal record of 11–30–1 over three years, from 1972 through 1974.

So it was up to Pardee to turn the team around, and Payton (who became a Bear the same year Pardee became head coach) was his ticket to success. If Pardee and players such as Payton succeeded in revitalizing the team, the Bears stood a chance of becoming a championship organization. However, in 1975, this prospect seemed far off. Sportswriter Mike Towle commented, "The path was wide open for Payton, although it would mean joining a team down in the dumps with a playoff berth likely light-years away."

MOVING TO CHICAGO

Although he was eager to start his NFL career, Payton missed his first two weeks of training camp because he injured his elbow while playing in the Senior Bowl, a college all-star game. When he finally arrived in Chicago, he was pleased to be there—but also nervous and unsure of himself.

The Windy City, as Chicago is called, was new to him. He had never lived in such a large, urbanized place. Nor had he spent any time in the North. Payton was used to the South's warm weather and slow pace of life. He knew that life in big, northern, industrialized Chicago was going to be a huge culture shock.

So, when he first arrived, Payton was even more reserved than usual—and more than a little intimidated. There was a lot to learn for a young man from small-town Mississippi. Bill

Magrane, one of the top executives in the Bears organization, tells a story that illustrates this point. Magrane was Payton's host at a welcoming dinner when the rookie arrived in Chicago. The executive recalled, "We were in a real fancy French restaurant with a menu this tall and everything in French. Payton looked at the menu and looked and looked, and the waiter finally came around, and Payton said, 'You got anything that's you know, like, just a piece of meat with nothing on it?'"

However, Payton was not the only Bears rookie to experience culture shock after moving to the big city. Roland Harper, Payton's close friend and (until injury forced his early retirement) one of his backfield mates on the Bears, was a native of Shreveport, Louisiana. Both he and Payton thus grew up in the Deep South. Consequently, the two players leaned on each other when they had to acclimate to life in Chicago. Commenting on their first impression of the Windy City, Harper said:

> Looking at all the tall buildings and being that we were both country boys, we tried to figure out how much hay could fit in those big tall buildings. It was a great shock to our systems. We were in awe when we came to Chicago to see the city.

ADJUSTING TO LIFE IN THE BIG CITY

He may have been intimidated at first, but Payton quickly adjusted. He got used to life in Chicago and grew to love it, even the city's notorious winds and winter snows. In his autobiography, Payton joked, "I have a big coat collection now." More important, he came to fiercely love the people of Chicago.

Still, that first season was tough. It helped that Payton's mother moved temporarily to Chicago to be a housekeeper for him during training camp. Alyne cooked, cleaned, and did whatever else she could to make her son's adjustment to city life easier. When training camp ended, she went back home to

Mississippi, although she continued to visit often during the regular season.

Meanwhile, Payton's steady girlfriend, Connie, felt sorry for him being all alone in a cold, unfamiliar city. She could not move there herself, however. For one thing, she was still a college student in Jackson. For another, she and Payton were not yet married. Their conservative, deeply religious families would definitely not have approved of them living together.

Payton tried not to let the problems of adjusting to a new home affect his performance in training camp. He worked just as hard, or harder, than he ever had. He was determined to prove that he could do well with an NFL team. Payton did indeed make a strong impression on his fellow Bears. The veterans on the team quickly realized that he was going to be a force to be reckoned with. **Linebacker** Doug Buffone recalled, "The first time I hit him in practice, I thought I had hit a brick wall."

"ZERO YARDS!"

Despite his relentless efforts to prepare himself during training camp, Payton's first NFL game was not an exceptional one. It was the Bears' season opener at Chicago's Soldier Field. Payton had only eight carries in that game, and he gained exactly zero yards. The team as a whole also had a bad day, losing to the Baltimore Colts, 35-7.

After that humiliating first game, Bill Magrane and his wife happened to walk next to Payton as they all left the stadium. Magrane started to introduce his wife to the rookie when they noticed he was crying. Magrane recalled, "He had some tears running down his cheeks, and my wife saw him and you know she reached over and patted him on the arm and she said things will get better. And of course things did get better. The next week he rushed for a hundred yards and that was that."

The game that day was an important lesson for Payton. Even though things got better—much, much better—he never forgot the humiliation he felt after that first game. He used the memory to spur himself on to greater achievements. The running back later remarked that for the rest of his career he often said to himself at crucial moments, "Zero yards!"

"EXCUSE ME, AN ANKLE!"

As Magrane's wife predicted, Payton's performance against the Colts was an aberration. Even before that game, he showed his talent. The first game he started—the team's next-to-last preseason game—was against the Miami Dolphins. He performed well, playing for three quarters and racking up the highest single-game total of the preseason.

He continued to improve throughout the season, and the public noticed. Besides appreciating his steadily improving statistics, Da Fans especially liked Payton's strong work ethic and his willingness to play even if he was hurt. Chicago fans were beginning to notice that the rookie from Jackson State was one tough guy, a workhorse who did a solid job without thinking too much of himself.

Overall, however, the 1975 season was a disappointment, for the Bears as a unit and for Payton personally. The team ended that year with a dismal record of 4–10. Payton had carried the ball only 196 times for 679 yards during the season, an average of just 3.5 yards per carry, and had scored only seven touchdowns.

Worse, Payton had to sit out one game—the one and only time, in four years of college and 13 seasons with the Bears, that he would miss a game. It happened because Coach Pardee was concerned about Payton's sore ankle. Payton wanted to tape the ankle and play anyway, as he had in college. Playing in every game was as important to him in the NFL as it had been in college. However, Pardee overruled him. For the rest of his career, the athlete never considered that game to be one missed due to injury, because he had been willing and ready. He later commented, "Excuse me, an ankle! . . . I'm going to set the record straight. If you're ready to play and the coach won't let you, is that a missed game?"

PERFECTING A DISTINCT STYLE

All through that rookie season, as he had in college, Payton continued to work on various techniques that could set him apart from other players. Because he was by no means the biggest player in the NFL, he knew he had to find ways to compensate. One way was to focus on increasing his power and quickness.

His years of punishing individual workouts helped in this regard, because he developed enormously powerful leg muscles. These amazing muscles gave Payton his characteristic stiff-legged, high-stepping running style. Another aspect of Payton's unusual running style was that it helped him avoid injury. When he ran, he deliberately planted only the balls and toes of his feet on the ground, keeping his heels high. That way, if someone hit him from the side on the leg, that leg could pivot freely and protect his knees from injury.

Another area of focus for Payton was his aggressive play. He loved the physical contact of football, so he continued to avoid running out of bounds. On the contrary—he frequently ran toward tacklers when he could have found open field instead, and he stiff-armed them nearly as often as he dodged them. He once knocked two defenders unconscious on a single running play. This aggressive style of play affected the opposition in more ways than one. Former Green Bay **center** Larry McCarren, who is now the team's radio color commentator and a member of the Packers Hall of Fame, believed Payton's mere presence could go far toward affecting the opposing team's psyche. He said:

> Insofar as Walter's effect on our team, it was devastating in the sense that he was one of the few guys I ever saw . . . who could actually, individually wear a team down. So often . . . it seemed like after three quarters, Walter would have something like forty-eight or fifty-two yards, and the defense would be thinking about

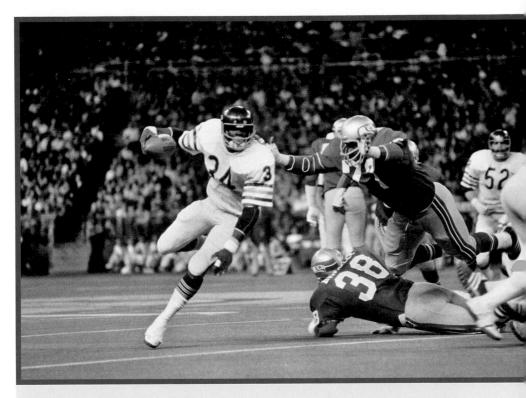

Known for his high-stepping running style, Walter Payton was able to avoid injury because he only planted the balls and toes of his feet on the ground when he ran. Consequently, when he was hit from the side, his leg would automatically pivot and not get caught in the turf. Here, Payton shows his unique running style in a game against the Seattle Seahawks in December 1976.

how we had done such a great job of containing him. And then in the fourth quarter, he explodes for a hundred and a half.

Payton's philosophy in this regard was simple: He wanted to punish any defender who wanted to bring him down. By doing so, he established himself as a hard-nosed football player who was not afraid to take a hit. He commented, "Why should I be the only one who gets clobbered? I try to neutralize the other player's attack by attacking him. . . . If you don't explode into him, by the laws of physics you're gonna take most of the impact."

MORE NOTABLE HABITS

Still another area where Payton worked hard was the goal-line leap—that is, scoring a touchdown by making a last-second jump over defenders into the end zone. He excelled at this; his

LEARNING TO BE A PRO

At only 5'10" and about 200 pounds, Walter Payton was smaller than many of his teammates and opponents on the field. He had to learn how to overcome his diminutive size, and, after joining the Chicago Bears, he worked on perfecting some of his techniques. Although he felt the burden of carrying the team on his shoulders during his rookie season in 1975, he was eager to learn everything he could from his teammates and simply by playing the game he loved. In their book, *Payton*, Connie, Brittney, and Jarrett Payton described Walter's on-the-job training:

Payton was learning to work with his blockers—to anticipate the holes they would tear open for him in an opposing team's defense. He was learning to smell the oncoming **blitz** in the air like a gathering thundershower. In a 31-3 shelling in San Francisco, he learned about the irresistible onslaught of a great passing game. In the snows of Green Bay, he learned how to keep fighting when it seemed like his very soul was frozen inside himself. He was finding his abilities, pushing his envelope, testing himself and his opponents. He was learning how to play his game at a professional level.

legs were so powerful that he could even leap into the end zone over defenders who were standing straight up.

And, though he never cheated, Payton was not above being a little sneaky at times. Early in his career, he had developed the habit of extending his arms as far forward as possible at the end of every carry. This moved the ball forward a few inches each time. During the course of a game, these tiny increments added up significantly.

Payton also got into the habit of standing up as soon as possible after being tackled. Partly, this was simply to show off his toughness—to prove that he was able to get up right away. But there was a more important reason: He was concerned about the dirty play that sometimes occurs after a tackle. He wanted to get away from these pileups quickly, thus lowering the chances that defenders might "accidentally" injure his ankles or knees.

Furthermore, Payton worked hard on developing his knack for finding holes and slipping past defenders. On many occasions, it would seem that he had been stopped cold—only to slip through a line of defenders to get free. At least one opponent had a theory, only half-joking, that Payton secretly sprayed his uniform before games with silicone (a material used to make nonstick cooking utensils), thus making himself too slippery to tackle.

STARTING DOWN THE ROAD TO GREATNESS

By working to perfect these distinctive moves, and his overall game, Payton steadily improved during the course of his rookie season. He was quickly learning how to play the game at a high level, and how to become part of an NFL team. And in the last game of the season, he finally had a chance to shine.

The Bears trounced the New Orleans Saints, 42-17, and Payton personally had a great game. He rushed for 134 yards on 25 carries, scored a 25-yard touchdown, caught 5 passes for 62 yards, and returned two **kickoffs** totaling 104 yards. It was the most exciting performance by a Chicago running back since the glory years of Gale Sayers.

Payton's personal life was going well, too. In July 1976, he married Connie in a quiet, low-key ceremony. Connie moved to Chicago after the wedding and enrolled in school there, because she had not yet finished college.

However, the positive aspects of Payton's life were not enough for him. He was discouraged about his overall performance and worried that he might not be a star for the Bears. But the older, more experienced players on the team told him to hang tough.

They assured Payton that his time would come—and it did. As he improved as a player and began to become an integral part of the Bears organization, he started to emerge as a natural leader and role model both on the field and off. In the years to come, Payton would become a crucial member of a team that finally found its focus and started down the road to greatness.

Moving on Up

True to the predictions of the Bears' veteran players, Walter Payton's second season was a big improvement. He rushed for 1,390 yards on 311 carries (a 4.5-yard average) and scored 13 touchdowns that season. His outstanding performance put him only slightly behind the league's leading rusher, O. J. Simpson of the Buffalo Bills, who ran for 1,503 yards in 1976.

Things got even better during Payton's third season. He carried the ball 339 times for a career-high 1,852 yards (a 5.5-yard average) and 14 touchdowns, during what was then a 14-game season. That season, he earned the NFL MVP Award, becoming the youngest player to date to receive that honor.

Perhaps his finest performance during that third season was a spectacular 40-carry, 275-yard game against the Vikings.

On November 20, 1977, Walter Payton set an NFL single-game record for rushing yards when he put together an amazing 40-carry, 275-yard effort in a 10-7 win against the Minnesota Vikings at Soldier Field. The record would stand for nearly 23 years, until Cincinnati tailback Corey Dillon ran for 278 yards in October 2000.

This set an NFL record for the most yards gained in a single game—a record that stood for 23 years, until it was broken by just three yards in 2000 by Corey Dillon (then with the Cincinnati Bengals). Not only was it an amazing performance and an outstanding game, but Payton had the flu that day and played despite his illness.

Payton's statistics continued to hold steady or improve during the next few years. The exception was 1982, and that was not his fault. That year, NFL players went on strike because they were unhappy with contract negotiations and salary levels. The strike lasted for 57 days and shortened the season, so there were only nine games that year. The Bears' record that season was 3–6, and

Payton rushed for only 596 yards on 148 carries. Even so, he surpassed a major personal goal: 10,000 career rushing yards.

Payton's rapid improvement and better performance throughout the late 1970s and early 1980s earned him more money. By 1980, he was earning $450,000 per season. His salary made him the highest-paid player in the league. By comparison, the average salary for an NFL athlete at the time was a mere $117,000 per season.

INDIVIDUAL PERFORMANCE

There are probably several reasons behind Payton's steady improvement. One may have been that he was now a married man; with Connie keeping him company in Chicago, he was not as lonely and had a rewarding personal life. However, much of his improved performance was probably simply a reflection of his overall greater skill as an athlete and the confidence he had in his teammates. He was learning to fit in, as well as steadily improving the strengths that made him a distinctive player, and it showed.

Sweetness never stopped working to improve himself as a well-rounded, jack-of-all-trades football player. Running and blocking were still his strengths, as they always had been, but Payton worked hard to be versatile in other ways as well. This

MOST RUSHING YARDS GAINED IN AN NFL GAME

NUMBER	PLAYER
296	Adrian Peterson, Minnesota vs. San Diego, November 4, 2007
295	Jamal Lewis, Baltimore vs. Cleveland, September 14, 2003
278	Corey Dillon, Cincinnati vs. Denver, October 22, 2000
275	Walter Payton, Chicago vs. Minnesota, November 20, 1977

often paid off. For instance, in one game against the Vikings in 1979, he ran for, passed for, and caught a touchdown—a feat that only six other players in NFL history have performed. He even played quarterback for one game in 1984.

Meanwhile, Payton continued to refine his unique style. For example, he worked hard to improve his stutter step. He knew that he was quick on short runs but did not have break-away speed. He could easily gain 30 or 40 yards, but if he had to run for 60 or 70 yards, he knew there was a greater chance of being caught.

The stutter step helped solve this problem by making his movement unpredictable at any given moment. If an opponent could be faked out by a false step, finding it impossible to pre-dict where Payton was going, that opponent would not have time to adjust to Sweetness's change of direction. Naturally, this made him harder to catch.

BECOMING A LEADER

During this time, Payton still did much of his training by him-self. He continued to do the same punishing kinds of workouts he had always done on his own, because he needed to set his own pace. Connie Payton remarked, "He understood [that] the only one he had control over was him."

But Payton also knew well that football is a team sport. The results can be disastrous if a team does not work together as a single, focused unit. So he also concentrated on fitting in with the team as a whole. In so doing, he began to emerge as a natural leader.

Other players began to look at him as a role model in almost every situation. **Wide receiver** Willie Gault remarked, "He had great leadership, unspoken leadership most of the time. He led by example on and off the field." This influence extended far beyond his own team; according to Green Bay quarterback Brett Favre, who idolized Payton as a child: "Even if you weren't a running back, Payton was still the guy you looked up to for how to be a team player and also [to be] just a good guy, on and off the field."

A REAL JOKER

One of the attributes that made Payton a natural leader was his humor. As he had done throughout his life, Sweetness frequently used humor to encourage his teammates when they

"HE'S A GAMECHANGER"

Having a running back as talented as Walter Payton can mean everything to the quarterback in a game—the difference between victory and defeat. Three-time NFL MVP Brett Favre, the Green Bay Packers' star quarterback, has accomplished a great deal during his 17-year career. He has played in two Super Bowls (winning one), is a nine-time Pro Bowler, has started every game for the Packers since he first suited up for the team in 1992, and has the most wins by a quarterback in NFL history (160). Despite all of these accomplishments, Favre has never had the opportunity to play with a running back who was anywhere close to being as talented as Walter Payton. Favre had this to say about Payton, a player he idolized when he was growing up in Mississippi:

> I can tell you what it means to have a running back like Walter Payton carrying the football for you. A guy with that kind of talent alters the whole face of the game. He shifts the dynamic of everything that's going on out on that field. He takes an enormous amount of pressure off of the quarterback. He gives you more control over the clock, more control over possession. A player like Walter isn't just a game saver, he's a gamechanger.

were playing poorly—and during these years, poor performances were happening far too often. **Fullback** Roland Harper recalled of Payton, "During even the toughest years, when we couldn't buy a win, he'd always make everyone laugh."

On one occasion, fullback Matt Suhey dropped a pass during a game against the Colts. He was clearly dejected about the botched play as the players made their way back to the **huddle**. Payton lightened the situation by teasingly "comforting" Suhey, saying, "You can always get a paper route or join the army."

Payton's sense of humor stayed with him off the field as well. When the team traveled to different cities, for instance, he often struck up conversations with people who did not recognize him. Sometimes, for his own amusement, he told them with a straight face that he was a male stripper.

But Payton also had a serious side to his personality, especially if it involved failure on the football field. If another Bear performed poorly, such as missing a block that led to Payton being tackled too soon, Payton had a way of quietly making his feelings known. This usually took the form of a silent but powerful stare; offensive tackle Keith Van Horne recalled: "If you got the stare; you knew you did something wrong or you better do something right."

ALMOST WICKED

Payton's love of practical jokes also stayed with him during these years. Despite his reputation for being a sweet guy, his jokes often seemed to border on wickedness. For example, he liked to set off firecrackers in the middle of the night during training camp, rudely awakening exhausted teammates who were trying to sleep after twice-daily practices.

Once, he set off a firecracker during the night in training camp and the police and fire departments arrived. The other players knew just who to blame, and the authorities went to Payton's room to confront him. By the time they got there, though, he had sneaked out a window and somehow managed to set off the sirens on the police cars.

On another occasion, after practice on an especially cold day, Payton ran back to the locker room ahead of everyone else. He locked the doors and took a long shower while the rest of the team was forced to stand around outside in the freezing cold.

Payton also sometimes used his high-pitched voice to play practical jokes on his teammates. He would call their numbers and pretend to be a girlfriend—thus making several wives furious. And he sometimes used his high voice to answer phones at Bears headquarters, pretending that he was a female secretary. Although he loved to clown around during practice and off the field, Payton never did so during a game—unlike some of today's players. *Chicago Tribune* sportswriter Don Pierson described Payton's ability to act like a professional during a game:

> He was really a cutup and a prank without being a showboat. He never did any of that stuff for the benefit of the fans or the cameras, like any of those end-zone dances or jumping up after making a run to make someone look bad. But in practice and stuff he was as crazy as any of these guys today who are doing it only for the camera. If he had taken any of that stuff from practice to the camera, he would have made [**cornerback** and notorious showoff] Deion Sanders look like a wallflower.

FRIENDS

As he settled into life as a Bear, Payton made some lasting friends. Roland Harper was Payton's best friend on the team throughout the running back's early years with the Bears. The two men came from similar backgrounds and had much in common. Both were from the South, both went to small colleges, and both loved to hunt.

But the fullback had serious knee problems and was forced to retire after the 1982 season. Payton was unhappy and worried about losing Harper's support on the field. Because of the positions they played, with Harper blocking for Payton, they had developed a superb working relationship. Payton commented, "I felt like a part of me was missing."

Fortunately, Harper's replacement, Matt Suhey, was up to the task, and he and Payton clicked despite some clear differences. For one thing, Suhey was white. Also, his college experience had been vastly different from Payton's; instead of toiling for a small and relatively obscure school, Suhey was the third generation in his family to play for powerhouse Penn State. Furthermore, he enjoyed talking to the media, unlike the notoriously press-shy Payton.

Nonetheless, as with Harper, Suhey and Payton became close friends and developed a close rapport on the field. Roland Harper recalled, "Walter liked people he didn't have to say a lot to. He liked people who just knew what he was thinking or where he was going. That overcame all the differences between Walter and Matt, because Matt grew to the point that he just knew Walter's thoughts."

Suhey was one of the first white people Payton became really close to. Their friendship was a positive example for the Bears, helping to smooth the occasional racial friction within the team. Suhey honored Payton by asking the running back to be godfather to his younger son. And they never seemed to tire of teasing each other, such as Sweetness's reference to Suhey as "a short, obnoxious Penn Stater" (even though the fullback was actually about an inch taller than Payton).

FANS

All throughout this period, Payton continued to be a favorite of Da Fans. They appreciated his nonstop effort, week in and week out, despite the team's dismal record—61–70 in Payton's first nine seasons. During those years, he stood head

While playing for the Chicago Bears, Walter Payton developed a close relationship with fullback Matt Suhey, who entered the league in 1980. The backfield duo became such good friends that Payton named Suhey the executor of his will when Payton became sick in the late 1990s. Suhey is pictured here during the 1984 NFC Championship against the San Francisco 49ers, a game the Bears would lose, 23-0.

and shoulders above the other Bears, but he never made a big deal out of it. Sportswriter Dan Brekke commented, "Payton's career was spent with a team that always seemed to find a way to make the least of his enormous talents."

Payton was not only popular with teammates and fans—even the fans of other teams liked him. For example, after a game in 1981 in which the Cowboys beat the Bears, the Dallas fans gave Payton a huge standing ovation as he walked off the field, because his performance had been outstanding.

For his part, Payton remained grateful for the continued support of fans, and he made sure he repaid them whenever possible. He could be stern with autograph seekers who abused the privilege—he disliked it when people wanted multiple signatures just so they could sell them later—but generally he always agreed to stop and sign autographs.

On many occasions, Payton went out of his way for his fans. A good example came after his playing days had come to an end, when he was attending a promotional event in a shopping mall. An elderly woman stood patiently in line for an autograph, but did not reach the front before the session had ended. Sweetness noticed her crying as she walked away. He asked a colleague to find her in the mall and then call Payton on a cell phone. Payton located her and learned that she wanted the autographs for her grandsons. He chatted with her for about 15 minutes and later sent a couple of signed footballs to her grandsons.

PERSONAL LIFE

When not appearing at such events or playing football, Payton had a full private life. He especially liked relaxing at the home he and Connie owned in the Chicago suburbs. But Payton also liked to get out in the country, as he had when he was a boy in Columbia. One of his favorite hobbies was hunting. He especially loved to go to a spot just across the Illinois border in Wisconsin. He and his friends who also hunted, including

Roland Harper and Matt Suhey, often took other players with them as an exercise in building team unity.

However, not everything in Payton's personal life during this period was positive. His father died in 1979 under somewhat strange circumstances. The elder Payton had been driving in Columbia one night when he was pulled over by a white police officer for driving erratically. Mr. Payton's balance and speech were not right, and the officer thought he had been drinking.

This was strange, because the elder Payton rarely drank; nonetheless, the policeman put him in a jail cell overnight. In the morning, he was found dead of a brain aneurysm. (An aneurysm is a sudden swelling of a blood vessel that is usually fatal if it bursts.) In retrospect, it seems likely that the aneurysm had already struck when Mr. Payton was arrested, affecting his balance and speech and making him seem drunk. However, because no one realized it, he never received medical attention.

The Payton family's sadness over this death was balanced by a happier event the following year. On the day after Christmas 1980, Payton's first child and only son, Jarrett, was born.

IRON MIKE RETURNS

Jarrett was born less than a week after Payton had wrapped up his sixth season with the Bears. During those six seasons, the team had not performed up to the standard set by Payton, but he remained loyal and never expressed any interest in being traded. He was happy in Chicago, and he liked his teammates and the fans.

He also dreamed of someday helping the Bears reach the playoffs, or even the Super Bowl. For years, of course, that dream seemed a long way off. This had been true while Jack Pardee was head coach, and it was true after Neill Armstrong replaced Pardee in 1978. However, in January 1982, the situation changed dramatically. That was when Mike Ditka became head coach.

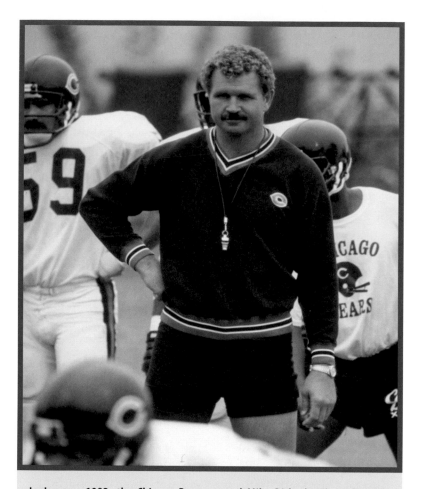

In January 1982, the Chicago Bears named Mike Ditka head coach. After a 3–6 campaign during the strike-shortened 1982 season and an 8–8 mark in 1983, Ditka righted the ship in 1984, leading Chicago to the NFC Championship Game. Ditka is pictured here at practice during his first season as Bears coach.

Ditka was a former Bear himself—he had been an outstanding **tight end** before going on to play for the Philadelphia Eagles and the Dallas Cowboys. After his retirement in 1972, "Iron Mike" had become an assistant coach for the Cowboys before returning to Chicago to coach the Bears. The effect on the team was immediate.

BELIEVING "LIKE WALTER DID"

Prior to Ditka's arrival, the Bears had had only two winning seasons out of their last 14. Iron Mike turned things around by making several important changes. For one thing, he helped develop an outstanding team—players of Payton's caliber. Among them were quarterback Jim McMahon, whom Ditka and the Bears drafted in the first round in 1982, linebacker Mike Singletary, defensive tackle Dan "Danimal" Hampton, and wide receiver Willie Gault, a first-round draft pick in 1983.

Just as crucial was Ditka's ability to pull these individuals together into a unit. He succeeded in getting them focused and working together toward becoming a championship organization. This was no simple task. For years, the Bears' defensive and offensive players had been antagonistic toward each other. Many observers had pointed out that the team never played as a single unit—they seemed to be playing against each other.

Much of the credit for this dramatic turnaround went to Ditka. However, the coach was quick to acknowledge the importance of Payton's contributions as well. In Ditka's opinion, Payton set the standard for the team with his hard work and positive attitude. The coach commented, "It had always been my lifelong dream to go back and coach the Bears. And to have a collection of guys like I had, I knew we had a great opportunity. We just needed to get everyone to believe like Walter did."

Payton was now on the verge of entering his glory years, the period of his greatest triumphs. He was about to achieve important personal records. And his beloved Bears were finally about to reign victorious in the biggest game of them all—the Super Bowl.

Seasons of Glory

Several important milestones marked Walter Payton's greatest years as a player—1984 and 1985. One was setting a new record for the all-time NFL career rushing mark. Sweetness bested the old record, 12,312 yards, set by Jim Brown, the legendary running back for the Cleveland Browns. Brown's record stood for more than two decades until Payton beat it.

Throughout the 1984 season, anticipation rose as Payton drew close to the old record. He told reporters, "I want to set the record so high that the next person who tries for it, it's going to bust his heart." But another outstanding player also was approaching it. This was Franco Harris, the Pittsburgh Steelers great who had recently signed with the Seattle Seahawks. Payton and Harris were friendly; their families socialized, and they even had some business dealings together. But the news media, hoping to generate interest, made the race seem as though the two were in a fierce rivalry.

The competition was decided on October 7, 1984. The occasion was a Bears home game against the New Orleans Saints. Ironically, the stadium was not sold out that day even though "Da Fans" knew full well that Payton was close to breaking the record. This may have been because of stiff competition for the attention of sports fans; the Chicago Cubs were in the middle of the National League Championship series with the San Diego Padres.

BREAKING THE RECORD

Although it was an important moment, Payton's triumph came during a relatively unimportant play: a simple six-yard run on the second carry of the second half. Bears executives had planned a brief ceremony to mark the moment, but Payton vetoed that plan. He did not want to attract too much attention. *Sports Illustrated* writer Rick Telander commented, "When Payton's moment of glory came, he wanted the game to continue. He rose from the pile of New Orleans tacklers . . . ready to run again."

Instead of a big ceremony, there was simply an announcement to the crowd, and Payton shook a few hands and slapped a few high fives. The celebrations came later: That night, the athlete's mother cooked his favorite dishes for a dinner at the Payton house. And in the days that followed, there was public fanfare as well, including congratulatory phone calls from Jim Brown and President Ronald Reagan.

In honor of his achievement, the Bears gave Payton a hefty bonus, and one of his sponsors presented him with an expensive sports car—a canary-yellow Lamborghini. During the ceremony when he received the sports car, the Bears' stadium parking lot was packed with photographers and reporters. At one point, Walter, who was notoriously shy around the press,

Walter Payton celebrates with teammate Todd Bell after becoming the NFL's all-time leading rusher during the Bears' 20-7 win over the New Orleans Saints on October 7, 1984. Payton finished his career with 16,726 yards rushing, and his record was not broken until former Cowboys running back Emmitt Smith eclipsed the mark in 2002.

put his young son, Jarrett, in the car, using the occasion to get away from the crowd and have a quiet talk. Jarrett commented later, "It's like he just shut out all of the madness and took time out to chill with me in the front seat." Despite the enjoyable father-son time spent with Jarrett, Walter soon got rid of the car. It was too showy for his taste.

To reporters, Payton downplayed the event. He said it was unfair to compare what he had done with Brown's achievement. He pointed out that he played longer and played more games than Brown had. Despite Payton's humility, Brown was glad that Walter and not Franco Harris had broken his record. After all, Brown had openly criticized Harris's habit of running out of bounds to avoid opponents. He preferred Payton's style, which was to meet them head-on. Brown commented, "I had a lot of respect for Walter when he broke the record. . . . I was very happy to acknowledge him. . . . Some people I would not have talked to because I would not have had that level of respect."

According to Bears head coach Mike Ditka, Payton was so confident of breaking Jim Brown's all-time career rushing record that, when it finally happened, it was no big deal. Ditka said, "When he broke the record he didn't say very much at all. It was really subtle. They stopped the game, gave him the ball, everybody gave him a standing ovation. I know that was something he wanted to do, and I don't think after he did it that he thought it was the most important thing. I think he expected to do it." Furthermore, Payton said, records were made to be broken. He was happy to set a new one, but he knew that someday his would be surpassed, too. He joked, "As far as anybody coming along and breaking that record, I have no quarrels about it. Just as long as it's my son."

REACHING THE PLAYOFFS

In addition to Payton's wonderful accomplishment, the Bears themselves achieved something that the team had not done

MOST RUSHING YARDS IN NFL HISTORY

YARDS	PLAYER
18,355	Emmitt Smith, Dallas, 1990–2002; Arizona, 2003–2004
16,726	Walter Payton, Chicago, 1975–1987
15,269	Barry Sanders, Detroit, 1989–1998

since 1979: They made the playoffs. More important, they captured their first division title since 1963, when they won the NFL championship. In the divisional round, the team traveled to Washington, D.C., to play the Redskins, the defending NFC champions. Payton set the pace by rushing for 104 yards, and the Bears won, 23-19. But then the team went up against the team that would go on to win the Super Bowl that season, the San Francisco 49ers, and it was a disaster—the final score was a humiliating 23-0.

Thus ended the Bears' chances to win their first championship since 1963. For Payton and the rest of the team, it had been thrilling to come so close to reaching the Super Bowl, but devastating to be crushed so badly. Payton later commented on that high and low, "The greatest feeling that I ever had in football and the worst feeling that I ever had in football were a week apart."

A discouraged Payton thought it might be another 10 years before the Bears had another chance at reaching the Super Bowl, long after his retirement. But linebacker Wilber Marshall told him to cheer up, because 1985 would be their year. Marshall said, "Next year, we're not going to just knock on the door, we're going to kick the damn door down."

"THE RIGHT MIX"

By the start of the 1985 season, it was clear that Payton and the rest of the team shared this attitude. That year's edition of the Bears boasted, besides Sweetness, Suhey, and Marshall, a number of gifted athletes who, singly and together, reached new levels of intensity and purpose. Among them were Jim McMahon, Willie Gault, Mike Singletary, **safety** Gary Fencik, **defensive end** Richard Dent, and defensive tackles Steve McMichael, Dan "Danimal" Hampton, and William "The Refrigerator" Perry.

Even during the preseason, it became clear that this team was unusually strong, cohesive, and optimistic. The group was a study in contrasts. It had wild characters (such as McMahon with his Mohawk haircut), but it also had steady, unassuming players such as Walter Payton. Payton worked hard to keep this varied group of individuals focused, both on and off the field. Matt Suhey commented,

> He wasn't just the best player on the field, he was the best leader off of it. That team would have exploded had there not been Walter there to keep it together . . . . All the chemicals were there for an explosion, and Walter proved he could instead turn it into the right mix.

"AMERICA'S TEAM"

The season started off well—a 38-28 win at home over Tampa Bay—and from then on the 1985 Bears could do no wrong. Da Fans went wild, and football followers throughout the country were also riveted. This was partly because the team played so well, of course, but it also was because they were obviously having fun, too. This sense of fun made them magnetically attractive, as Connie Payton recalled:

> That team was really a great group. They were fun to watch and had so much personality and character. You just don't see that anymore. You fell in love with every-one on the team. . . . It was amazing how it all kind of took off. They were America's team.

The team knew it was hot. In fact, the Bears were so enthusiastic about their chances of winning it all that they recorded a music single and video, "Super Bowl Shuffle," before they were even assured a playoff berth. Fans throughout the country responded with equal enthusiasm; "Super Bowl Shuffle" became a best seller and was nominated for a Grammy Award. Ironically, in the video, Payton and quarterback Jim McMahon seem to float across the screen, separate from the rest of the team. This is because they were not available on the day the video was shot, so their images had to be superimposed later.

When that magical season ended, the Bears had a near-perfect record. Their only loss had been to the Miami Dolphins, in the thirteenth game, 38-24. In postseason play, the Bears also performed magnificently, beating the New York Giants, 21-0, in the divisional round of the playoffs, and the Los Angeles Rams, 24-0, in the NFC Championship Game. At long last, they were headed to the Super Bowl.

Even so, everyone in the Bears organization was bitter over that one loss to Miami. They were hoping to see the Dolphins again in the Super Bowl so they could exact revenge. But the **American Football Conference (AFC) wild-card** team, the New England Patriots, upset Miami, 31-14, in the AFC Championship Game—which made it a Bears-Patriots matchup for Super Bowl XX.

A SMASHING VICTORY

That game, played in New Orleans on January 26, 1986, was a stunning victory for the Bears, in several ways. First of all, they won. But they did not simply win—they smashed the Patriots with the most lopsided Super Bowl score in NFL history: 46-10.

Several other records were set or equaled that day. The Bears established a new Super Bowl record for the most points scored by a team. (The previous record was 38, shared by the San Francisco 49ers in Super Bowl XIX and the Los Angeles Raiders in Super Bowl XVIII.) The Bears' defense also tied a Super Bowl record for **sacks** (seven). And they held the Patriots to a record-low seven rushing yards. Furthermore, Mike Ditka became only the second man to win a Super Bowl ring as both a player and as a coach. (Tom Flores of the Raiders was the other.)

However, Super Bowl XX was a bittersweet victory for Walter Payton. He was unable to shine, because the New

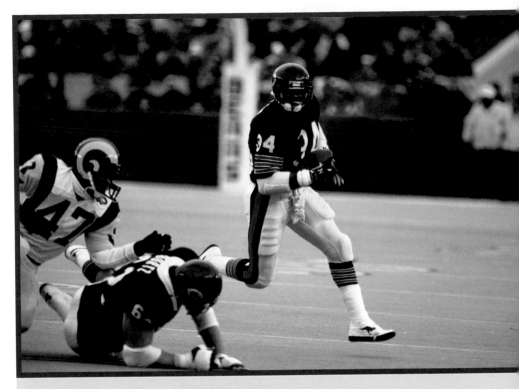

Walter Payton breaks to the outside during the Bears' 24-0 win over the Los Angeles Rams in the NFC Championship Game on January 12, 1986. That season, Payton rushed for more than 1,500 yards in helping to lead Chicago to its first Super Bowl appearance in franchise history.

England defense focused on stopping him. In fact, it seemed at times as though the Patriots' entire purpose on the field was to stifle Sweetness. Connie, Brittney, and Jarrett Payton wrote, "It became clear that New England's defense . . . was there for one man and one man only. In the way they tracked him, shadowed him and followed him, the Pats' defensive line seemed to think that Payton was the entire Chicago team."

BAD NEWS AND GOOD NEWS

The Patriots' focus on keeping Payton in check was both bad news and good news for the Bears. The bad news was that

Sweetness was able to rush for only 61 yards on 22 attempts, a fraction of Chicago's 408 total yards for the game. Even worse, he did not score a single touchdown.

However, the good news was that the Patriots' single-minded focus on Payton enabled the rest of the Bears to hurt New England. They gleefully took advantage of this freedom to make some amazing plays. Perhaps the most spectacular was Jim McMahon's 60-yard pass to Willie Gault—a play that signified that the Bears could do whatever they wanted to on offense. Throwing from his own end zone on **first down**, McMahon faked a **handoff** to Payton, then hit a streaking Gault to start a nine-play, 96-yard **drive** that gave the Bears an overwhelming 30-3 lead in the third quarter.

Payton understood well that the team came first. He knew that the Bears' triumph had been a group effort by what he called "a perfect team"—one that he was proud to be part of. Still, he was furious at not having had a chance to score. It was perhaps the most frustrating day of his life—a bitter disappointment for someone who had waited his entire career for that moment.

BITTER DISAPPOINTMENT

At first, Sweetness refused to meet the press after the game, but in time he was able to control his anger. As Bill Magrane recalled, "Walter wasn't going to go on TV, he was all bent out of shape. . . . He was hot. But he went [on air] and said all the right things. He did what he was supposed to do."

Several people who were there noted that Payton was not able to hide his disappointment. He told reporters that he was happy with the game's outcome, but the frustration of the day was nonetheless visible in his eyes. And in the days afterward, in the press and elsewhere, Coach Ditka was soundly criticized for not giving Payton an opportunity to score.

For his part, Ditka says he has always regretted the way the game turned out. He says he was so focused on winning

Although the Chicago Bears dominated the New England Patriots, 46-10, in Super Bowl XX, Walter Payton was held in check. He rushed for just 61 yards on 22 attempts (2.7 yards per carry) and did not score a touchdown in the otherwise glorious moment for the Bears.

that he never realized Payton had not scored a touchdown. The coach remarked, "That was probably the most disturbing thing in my career. That killed me. If I had one thing to do over again, I would make sure Payton took the ball into the end zone."

LETDOWNS AND GOOD TIMES

After that magical 1985 season and their Super Bowl victory, almost anything would have been anticlimactic for the Bears. Indeed, the 1986 season, although successful, was a bit of a letdown. It started well, with the Bears winning seven of their first eight games, and ended with another NFC Central Division title and an outstanding record of 14–2. But the team lost in the divisional round of the playoffs, falling to the Redskins, 27-13.

The reasons for underachieving in 1986 were never clear. Some observers felt that it was because Jim McMahon, the Bears' star quarterback, suffered a separated shoulder in Week 12 that ended his season, and the team had no replacement who was his equal. But Payton always felt the real reason was that the team's desire to win was simply gone.

In his opinion, the drive to the Super Bowl changed some of his teammates. After the Super Bowl triumph, some of the second-string players began lobbying for more playing time, and many of the Bears wanted a higher profile: more money-making endorsements, more ego-boosting interviews. Success, in his opinion, had wrecked the Bears' focus.

The 1986 season was a disappointment for Payton professionally, but it was a good year for him personally. His and Connie's second child, a daughter named Brittney, had been born in 1985, and Payton was having a great time watching her and Jarrett grow up. He especially liked taking photos of them, bringing them presents from his travels, and playing with them. Brittney later recalled, "He was always playing jokes and had us rolling on the ground laughing. He was always a prankster."

That year also marked the Paytons' 10-year anniversary. Their wedding had been quiet and modest, but Walter knew that Connie had always wanted something bigger. So he arranged a surprise ceremony on their anniversary, secretly flying in a number of people who were important in Connie's life—including the minister from the church she had attended as a girl. He managed to keep this elaborate surprise completely hidden from her until it was time to spring it.

SLOWING DOWN

The following year, 1987, Payton signed a one-year, $1 million contract with the Bears. It was the first single-year contract he had ever signed; all his others had been three-year commitments. This showed that Bears management was not willing to make a long-term commitment to Payton. After a dozen superb years, Payton was finally showing signs of wear and tear, and Bears management was not sure how much longer he could play.

It goes without saying that football players, especially running backs, have a short shelf life. It has been estimated that Payton was tackled about 7,000 times during his NFL career. But he also was famous for staying on the field no matter what. For the last few years of his career, he had been playing brilliantly despite suffering from, at various times, broken ribs, a separated shoulder, a severely sprained ankle, and bad knees. Connie, Jarrett, and Brittney Payton reflected: "No player took more hits and complained less; few played with more pain game to game." There were no magic remedies that helped Payton overcome the ongoing pain. He always said that his amazing ability to withstand pain, day in and day out and year after year, was simply to find a way past it. He reflected:

> When you have pain, what you do is you focus on non-pain. You focus your mind on soothing. You focus your mind on creating a healing form. I've had injuries that for some people would have taken them three and four weeks to heal from, but with me it would only take three and four days. The reason I healed quickly is that I didn't dwell on the pain.

Sometimes Sweetness would be so banged up after a game that he could barely move. His friend Joe Kane recalled, "I would have dinner with him the Monday after a game or whatever, days when he couldn't raise his right arm up even to drink a cup of coffee, and he would be doing everything left-handed."

All of this physical contact took its toll. Inevitably, Payton was slowing down, he was not as agile as he had once been, and his rushing totals were beginning to decline. Matt Suhey commented, "I don't want to say he lost his step, but physically I think he had taken a beating over the years. And there [were] probably some people as good as he was at that point."

BOWING OUT

More and more, the Bears' executives began making it clear that they wanted to phase Payton out. They drafted a new running back, Neal Anderson from the University of Florida. For a while, Ditka worked Payton and Anderson together in the same backfield, even though neither was a true fullback. That season, Anderson was the Bears' leading rusher in 8 out of 12 games.

Payton's business partner and agent, Bud Holmes, also was urging Sweetness to retire. Holmes wanted him to focus on something new. He wanted Payton to become the owner, or at least part owner, of an NFL franchise.

But Payton did not want to retire. He felt he had a couple of good years left in him. He later remarked, "I can tell you today, if it had been my choice, I wouldn't have retired. . . . I just kept saying, 'Two more years.'" But the pressure was strong; Payton finally gave in and decided to retire at the end of the 1987 season.

Payton began to regret the decision almost immediately. After all, he was only 33 years old and thought he could still play. He later said,

I was not ready to retire. I regret the fact that I listened to the counsel that was around me. Even in my last game, I had a great game. I was in incredible shape. I worked out all the time. I really, really felt that I could stay. But under the pressure of the people I chose to surround myself with, I was convinced that this was what I needed to do. So I didn't listen to myself; I didn't listen to my inner thoughts and how I really felt.

Nonetheless, Payton had made up his mind, and then he made his decision public. It was time to begin focusing on the next phase of his life—one that would no longer directly involve playing the game he loved.

Retiring
Number 34

The official end to Walter Payton's football career began at halftime during a game against the Seattle Seahawks on December 20, 1987. The Bears held a ceremony at halftime to retire the number 34, which had been Sweetness's number throughout his college and professional careers. Asked to speak to the crowd, Payton made a few simple and heartfelt comments. He said, "I came into this game because I loved to play, and because it was fun. It's still that way. Thank you for being here."

Chicago lost that day, 34-21, but the fans at Soldier Field hardly seemed to care. They were totally focused on Sweetness. As usual, the stands were dotted with dozens of handmade signs honoring the athlete and expressing Da Fans' love for him. Typical of these signs, seen from the time he had

On December 20, 1987, the Bears retired Walter Payton's number during a ceremony at halftime of Chicago's 34-21 loss to the Seattle Seahawks. Here, Payton thanks Bears fans for their unwavering support during his 13-year career.

announced his retirement, was one with a timely Christmas theme: SANTA: PLEASE SEND MORE WALTER PAYTONS. FIRST ONE WAS PERFECT.

ENTERING RETIREMENT

Sweetness's final game was a 21-17 loss to the Washington Redskins in the NFC divisional playoffs at Soldier Field. He rushed for 85 yards on 16 carries and had three catches for 20 yards. Long after that final contest ended, Payton stayed on the bench in full gear. He looked out at the field and remembered old games and old plays. Payton remarked later that he would have stayed there until the lights of the stadium were turned out, but he was touched by fans calling his name and went out to meet them.

And now it was time to move on. He was retired, and he had a new task: keeping busy without the regimentation of regular practices and games, a routine he had followed for his entire adult life. Many of his friends and family thought he would be happy just to rest and relax after so many years of punishing his body with running, playing, and working out. However, retirement proved to be less simple, and relaxing, than it might have seemed.

Some recently retired people have no trouble adjusting to this new phase of their lives. But Payton loved playing football, had never done anything else for a living, and found he needed something to fill that huge new void in his life. Plus, he was still the same energetic man he had always been. He had no desire to take it easy. Connie recalled: "He was someone who had to be busy. And yeah, it would drive me a little crazy sometimes. I'd say, 'Enjoy life,' but for him, that was enjoying life."

TRYING TO STAY BUSY

Because it was impossible for him to sit still, Payton had to find many different things to do. He did not really need to work anymore. He had been paid well, had invested his money wisely, and for the most part did not have lavish spending habits. Financially, therefore, he was comfortable. (He was, however, never rich by today's standards; even in his top earning years, Payton made less annually than an average NFL **starter** makes today.)

One way he occupied his time was to take part in a weekly show on a Chicago sports radio station. He also produced a few sports programs for the local Fox television affiliate. Typical of these was a show that asked offensive linemen questions such as: What gift would you like from a quarterback as a thank-you for protecting him? (Among the answers: jewelry and Ferraris.)

Payton also spent hours every day answering fan letters, which he received by the carload even in retirement. Kim Tucker, who worked for Sweetness, remarked,

> He loved sitting for hours and reading letters from his fans. Sometimes when a phone number was included in the letter he would call them. Upon reaching them you would have thought they won the Lotto. He would only talk ten to fifteen minutes per call, but it was always significant, and usually to a person that needed encouragement.

NO COACHING

Another way Payton stayed busy was to remain close to the Bears organization. He frequently visited the team's offices and sometimes, just for fun, manned the phones there. Also, the Bears' owners, the McCaskey family, invited him to join their board of directors.

Payton also got on the speaking circuit, frequently giving motivational speeches to meetings of companies and organizations. He enjoyed giving speeches, because he could reminisce about his glory days and talk about issues (such as hard work and commitment) that were important to him. Audiences liked Payton as well, because they could relate to his honest, down-to-earth attitude. His friend John Gamauf, an executive at Bridgestone/Firestone Tires, commented, "Not that Walter was the best motivational speaker—there's tons of motivational speakers out there. It's the way that he was so real about what he said."

Many retired athletes and other celebrities find second careers giving such speeches, and Payton liked talking to large groups on occasion. But he was never interested in something else other retired players often turn to: coaching. Part of the reason, he said, was that he could not understand other players' training programs, and he had no tolerance for laziness in others. Sweetness thought he would dislike coaching, because he wanted nothing to do with athletes who came to camp out of shape or who missed games and practices.

NEVER IDLE, ALWAYS FRIENDLY

In retirement, as earlier in his life, Payton was always in motion. His attention had always been pulled in several directions at once. This need for constant stimulation only increased for Payton when cell phones became popular. He was an early and enthusiastic user of cell phone technology, and his monthly bills often ran in the thousands of dollars.

However, he always preferred talking to people in person. In malls or other public places, Payton was always stopping to talk to someone, and he was equally friendly with everybody he met. Former Bears offensive lineman Dan Jiggetts recalled, "He was one of those guys who could walk through a lobby and go up to a doorman at the hotel or talk to the maid. His [feeling] was that everyone is important, not just executives and people like that."

Many years of life as a celebrity had taught the shy Mississippi boy to be friendly with everyone. This was true at least on a superficial level. On the other hand, he rarely opened up about his deeper feelings to anyone. Even his closest friend, Matt Suhey, commented, "He had a special gift for . . . making people feel comfortable. Joking around with waiters, giving those [kinds of] people the time of day. But when you got him one on one, to get close to him was difficult."

INVESTMENTS

Payton also kept busy in retirement by keeping an eye on his investments, of which he had several. He had grown up with great respect for people who owned small businesses, and he was always proud to invest in them. Over the years, he made some bad investments, but overall he made many good ones.

One of the good ones was McFadden Ventures, a company that managed nightclubs. Another was Walter Payton Power Equipment, which rented and sold heavy construction equipment. Yet another was Walter Payton's Roundhouse, a huge restaurant/brewpub complex in Aurora, Illinois, a suburb of Chicago.

Payton was a hands-on owner. He liked to be personally involved in any business that bore his name. For instance, he frequented the Roundhouse restaurant to talk with customers and staff, shaking hands and getting to know people. And he did not put on airs just because he was a celebrity owner; on at least one Christmastime evening, he donned an apron and served drinks to employees.

But one business plan overshadowed all of Payton's other retirement investments. This was something he had dreamed about for some time: owning, or at least partly owning, an NFL team. If successful, he would become the first African American to do so.

CHASING THE FOOTBALL FRANCHISE

Payton considered buying a stake in one of several teams, including the Los Angeles Raiders. But the most promising of these ventures seemed to be to bring an expansion team to St. Louis, Missouri (the St. Louis Cardinals had moved to Phoenix, Arizona, after the 1987 season). In 1989, Payton told a reporter for the *St. Louis Sun* that he saw this as a tremendous opportunity for everyone:

> I think owning a team would be as exciting as scoring touchdowns, but we're not just trying to fill our own pockets. This will benefit the whole community, area and state. With the desire that we have to do this the right way, all people will benefit.

Payton joined forces with several other businessmen to form a consortium that raised money and sought leadership. They spent years trying to bring a football franchise to St. Louis. But there was too much infighting within the group, and the project had trouble moving forward.

When NFL officials saw that the consortium was chronically troubled, they imposed a deadline by which the consortium had to create a single, workable plan. This deadline was not met, and the project finally fell apart. Payton commented later that, in his opinion, it collapsed simply because the consortium could not work together: "What killed that deal—five years of work—came down to three letters: E-G-O."

"A LONG STINT"

Eventually, in 1993, the NFL awarded expansion franchises to two cities (Jacksonville, Florida, and Charlotte, North Carolina), and St. Louis got a team when the Los Angeles Rams moved there in 1995. Meanwhile, Deron Cherry, a former strong safety for the Kansas City Chiefs, succeeded where Payton failed by buying part ownership in the Jacksonville franchise to become the first African-American owner in the NFL.

The collapse of the St. Louis project was a serious blow to Payton. He had turned down many business opportunities over the years to concentrate on it. More important, it was the first major goal he had set for himself that he could not complete.

To make matters worse, some of Payton's investments were not doing well during this period. He was forced to bring forth several lawsuits, including one against his former business manager and agent who had mismanaged Payton's funds. Connie remarked about her husband, "He believed you ought to be able to do business on a handshake basis. Unfortunately, not all of Walter's business partners felt the same way."

His business problems—especially the collapse of the St. Louis project—seriously depressed Payton. He became moody and stopped working out or doing other things that

THAT WOULD HAVE BEEN MY BABY

After the 1987 NFL season, the St. Louis Cardinals moved to Phoenix, Arizona, leaving the city without a professional football team. When the NFL announced in 1991 that it planned to add two expansion teams, St. Louis seemed a sure bet for a franchise, because it was the largest television market without an NFL team. Unfortunately, St. Louis had several ownership groups bidding for the franchise, which ultimately damaged the city's chances for acquiring a team. Walter Payton was involved with one such ownership group, which was led by Jerry Clinton, the major distributor for Anheuser-Busch beer in St. Louis County, Missouri. However, Clinton was not interested in becoming the majority owner, and after he was unsuccessful in his search to find a majority owner, the group had to bow out of the competition. When Payton's bid fell through, after years of hard work, he was crushed. He had passed up several good business opportunities to focus on becoming the first black owner of an NFL team. He later commented,

> I couldn't believe it. I was so sure of it. There were business offers that I turned down because I was sure I was going to be in the NFL. That was going to be my full-time focus. It would have been my baby, no question. Those business opportunities that came to me right after I retired never really came back. Four years after retiring, I wasn't as hot. Others stepped in and took my place.

gave him pleasure. At one point, he even filed for divorce. (Fortunately, this phase of his life was short lived; Connie patiently allowed him space to realize how much he needed and wanted to be near his family.) Payton's executive assistant commented that it "was a sad time for Walter, just trying to find himself. It was a long stint."

HALL OF FAME

Thankfully, Payton's depression lifted and he returned to his usual, positive self. This return to form was helped by several bright spots. One of the brightest was Sweetness's induction into the Pro Football Hall of Fame in Canton, Ohio. His stellar career had assured him of a place there long before he retired, and he was inducted in the first year of his eligibility, 1993.

Payton first asked Jim Finks to deliver the formal speech at his induction ceremony. Finks, the longtime general manager of the Bears, was the man who had been most responsible for drafting him in 1974. Payton held him in high regard. Unfortunately, Finks was seriously ill and was unable to attend the ceremony.

Payton then made a surprising choice: He asked his son, Jarrett, who was then 12 years old, to make the speech. Although he was nervous, Jarrett delivered it well, speaking movingly of his father as a role model, hero, and friend. He was the first person to introduce a parent at a Hall of Fame ceremony. Afterwards, an emotional Payton commented, "We made a wager of who would be the first one to break down in tears, and I was the first one to say that I wouldn't . . . [but] after hearing my son get up here and talk, I don't care if I lose the bet."

RACING

Another bright spot in his retirement years was Payton's continuing involvement in auto racing. Racing fulfilled his competitive spirit and helped lift his spirits. Besides, it was fun.

During his first year of eligibility in 1993, Walter Payton was inducted into the Pro Football Hall of Fame. Instead of having a former coach or teammate introduce him, Payton chose his 12-year-old son, Jarrett, to do the honors. Here, Jarrett and Walter hug after Jarrett introduced his father to those in attendance at the Hall of Fame induction ceremony on July 31, 1993.

His involvement in it grew from his love of cars, the faster the better. (Cautious friends knew better than to accept a ride from him, and his CB handle was "Mississippi Maniac.") Payton was very fussy about the cars he owned. They were detailed weekly, and no one was allowed to eat food in them. The Payton family always had eight or nine vehicles at any given time, including such luxury automobiles as a Rolls Royce and a Porsche.

From this general love of cars, it was a logical step to start racing them. Payton began on a small circuit of regional competitions, then moved up to a class of cars called GT-3, capable of speeds up to 140 miles per hour. For a time, Payton joined actor Paul Newman's team, Newman Racing. He traveled throughout the country to race with this team; he only won one race, but he had a lot of fun.

However, Sweetness stopped racing after he had a serious accident during a competition in Elkhart Lake, Wisconsin, in August 1993. He flipped over two fences, gas spilled from the car, and it caught fire. Payton was quickly pulled from the wreckage and was not badly hurt, although he had gas in his eyes, a burn on his neck, a mild concussion, and other minor injuries. Brittney, who was only seven at the time, was in the audience that day. She was terrified at witnessing her father's accident, and he promised to stop racing. After that, he settled for just owning his own team and for years was the only African-American owner in this white-dominated sport.

Auto racing always carries with it a certain element of danger. Even after his brush with death on the racetrack in Wisconsin, Payton loved to be around this atmosphere of risk. As he entered the next, and final, phase of his life, however, death came at him from a completely unexpected angle.

The End

The first signs that something might be wrong with Walter Payton's health appeared in the early 1990s. During a routine physical, doctors found that his liver enzyme levels were abnormal. But he was so healthy otherwise that neither Payton nor his doctors paid much attention.

Nothing more happened that was significant until the summer of 1998, when Payton noticed some stomach pain. Throughout his life, he had routinely ignored pain, however, so he did not take it seriously. He thought it was just food poisoning—perhaps, he guessed, from some bad crab.

That summer, Payton also seemed unusually tired. But he had a very busy schedule, often traveling four days a week on business. At first, he thought the fatigue was simply due to his demanding schedule.

But the stomach pain and tiredness never went away. By late summer, Sweetness was so fatigued that he could barely get through his weekly radio show. This was unusual, to say the least. Walter Payton, tired? Something was wrong.

BAD NEWS

Then other symptoms started appearing. He began to get acne, and the whites of his eyes turned yellow. Food tasted bland and smells bothered him, even familiar ones such as his after-shave lotion. Most alarming of all, he was quickly losing weight.

That fall, he agreed to enter one of the nation's top medical facilities, the Mayo Clinic in Rochester, Minnesota. However, he could not get an appointment until December. He decided to wait, rather than go elsewhere. The Mayo Clinic had a reputation as the best, which Payton appreciated, and he also valued its privacy policy.

Matt Suhey went with Payton to the clinic that winter. His old friend and former teammate was the only person Payton wanted to have with him when he visited the doctor. Suhey recounted this difficult time in Payton's life:

> I went to the hospital [with] him. And we checked him in under other names so no one would know he was there. He wanted to fight it by himself, and I think he had every right to do that. That's the way he wanted it. So I was going to uphold that.

The news Payton and Suhey received at the clinic was not good. Payton was diagnosed with primary sclerosing cholangitis (PSC), a rare disease that causes scarring and swelling of the bile ducts inside and outside the liver. (Bile is a substance that helps break down fat in the body. When it cannot move through, the liver becomes damaged.)

PSC has no known cause, and it is fatal. The doctors told Payton that his only chance of survival was a liver transplant.

With a transplant, he had a chance to make a full recovery. Without it, he would die within a year or two.

He was immediately put on a waiting list. Such lists are needed for organ transplants, because the number of people who need them is much greater than the number of available organs. These lists do not take into account celebrity status. Payton had no better chance than anyone else who was in need.

JARRETT'S PRESS CONFERENCE

Payton felt strongly about keeping his condition secret, believing that his health was his own business. Only he and a few family members and friends knew. Within weeks of his diagnosis, however, it became public knowledge.

The catalyst was a press conference his son, Jarrett, held in January 1999. By then a senior in high school, Jarrett was 6'2" and 210 pounds, and had been ranked the fifty-eighth best high school football player overall by *Sporting News*. A number of colleges had courted Jarrett, and he chose to attend the University of Miami. The purpose of the press conference was to announce this decision.

Walter was at Jarrett's side during the press conference. Despite Sweetness's desire to keep the focus on his son, someone asked why he was so thin. He joked that he was in training for a marathon. But that evening, a local television sports reporter, Mark Giangreco, compared Payton's gaunt appearance to that of Mahatma Gandhi. Payton was hurt and offended by this comment, and in the days afterward the question of his health was openly discussed by the media. Rumors developed that Payton had AIDS or was doing drugs.

Payton talked it over with his family and reluctantly decided to make a public announcement. Although he believed it was a private matter, he also thought he should quell the rumors:

> I felt this was nobody's business. Why couldn't this be
> a personal fight? Everyone was telling me the same

thing about needing to make things public. They said I had to do it because it wasn't fair; it wasn't fair to myself, and it wasn't fair to my family. People were starting to think it was AIDS or whatever, so my staff really sat down with me and said, "Walter, listen, this has to be addressed."

For Connie, Walter's decision to reveal his condition was a blessing; she hated keeping the knowledge secret. But for Walter, it was different: It was a painful decision for a man who had always refused to acknowledge weakness. Payton was proud of his abilities, and he never wanted to have anyone see him struggle with anything—not even something he could not control, such as a serious illness. Matt Suhey stated:

Physically, on the football field, he never wanted to be embarrassed. He never wanted to play poorly, he felt very strongly about that. If he **fumbled**, you could always rest assured he'd be ready to make the next play. He took extreme pride in that. He had a tremendous ego when it came to playing football, and I say that in a positive way. He'd never embarrass his work ethic.

SHOWING THE WORLD HOW TO FIGHT

The public announcement was made at a restaurant in suburban Rosemont, Illinois. For the occasion, Payton was dressed casually in sunglasses, black leather jacket, gray shirt, and jeans. His son was at his side.

After making his startling announcement, Payton was peppered with questions by reporters. Asked if he was scared, the athlete replied, "Am I scared? Hell yeah, I'm scared. Wouldn't you be scared? But it's not in my hands anymore. It's in God's hands." Asked if he had a message for the public, including those who might be spreading rumors about him, he said, "To

In December 1998, Walter Payton was diagnosed with primary sclerosing cholangitis (PSC), a rare disease that causes scarring and swelling of the bile ducts inside and outside the liver. Here, Payton breaks down at a February 2, 1999, news conference in Rosemont, Illinois, where he announced he needed a liver transplant. Behind him is his son, Jarrett.

the people that really care about me, just continue to pray. And for those who are gonna say what they want to say, may God be with you also."

Payton disliked talking to the press under the best of circumstances, and talking about his poor health was especially tough. Although he was clearly emotional during the press conference, Payton's optimism and determination to beat the illness also was evident. Mike Ditka later commented, "The one thing I told people after the press conference was that Walter would show us how to fight. He'll show everybody in the world how to fight."

In fact, everyone assumed that Payton would pull through. His son recalled, "All I could think in my head was, 'This is gonna get fixed. He'll be alright. He's Superman, he'll be fine.'"

"UNLESS A REAL HERO STEPS FORWARD"

The news made front-page headlines throughout the world, and the following weeks saw an overwhelming outpouring of support for Sweetness. Hundreds of thousands of letters came to Payton's office, and the office phone lines were jammed with people calling to wish him well.

Payton remained as active as possible during this period. In particular, he became an activist for organ donation. He knew that his celebrity status could help spread the word about the importance of this cause. So Payton appeared on several television talk shows, including *Larry King Live*, *The Oprah Winfrey Show*, and *CBS This Morning*, urging people to become donors. He also made a public service announcement connected with the program *Touched by an Angel*:

> For the past few weeks, *Touched by an Angel* has been exploring the true meaning of honor and courage. Along with me, over sixty thousand Americans are awaiting organ transplants. Only half of us will receive them unless a real hero steps forward like you. Please consider signing your donor card, and make sure you discuss this with your family. Thank you.

A TWIST OF FATE

All along, Payton had hoped a new liver would allow him to make a full recovery, but fate took another turn just a few weeks after his press conference. Doctors discovered cancer of the bile duct that had spread to his lymph nodes. Because the cancer was so advanced, Sweetness was ineligible for a transplant. A new liver would do him no good.

The news was a death sentence. Payton knew that without a new liver he did not have long to live. He tried to stay positive, continuing to speak out in support of organ donation even after he became ineligible. He was an organ donor himself, although he joked that, after 13 years as a professional football player, everything in his body was probably worn out.

Sweetness told friends that he was sure something good would come of his illness—perhaps it was that he could raise awareness about organ donation. It was a subject Payton remained passionate about. In his autobiography, written as he

TOUCHING LIVES

In February 1999, after Walter Payton announced he had been diagnosed with PSC (primary sclerosing cholangitis), hundreds of thousands of letters of support poured into his office. He realized he had met too many people in his time for him to remember them all—but that those people had not forgotten their meeting with him. After all, fans came to love Payton because he was not like the typical professional athlete. He was approachable and made himself accessible to all of his fans. He enjoyed joking around with them as if he was a longtime friend, and he was not above random acts of kindness, such as spending time with a dying child. Despite the fact that he touched so many people, Payton was overwhelmed at the outpouring of feeling he witnessed. He commented,

> When I was able to look at the hundreds of thousands of lives I've affected, I was blown away. Because, you know, you think, "Well, I went out of my way to go and speak to this person, oh, I did this." You'd think after all these years, they would have forgotten. I've gotten fan mail from people that I met fifteen years ago, and I still meant the same to them as the day I talked to them. I didn't realize—I really, for the first time, got it.

was dying, he commented, "If I can say anything in this book, it is *please* sign the donor's statement on the back of your driver's license; make sure you're listed as a donor with the right group in your state; and tell your family about your wishes."

WALTER AND MATT

As they had been when Payton was healthy and playing football, he and Matt Suhey remained close. Matt was the only person he allowed to take him to doctor appointments, and Payton made Suhey the executor of his will. This indicated that he trusted his friend absolutely to carry out his wishes after his death. Payton commented, "He didn't fail me on the field and he hasn't failed me since."

As Payton grew sicker, his friend more or less moved into the Payton house. The two spent hours watching sports on television, and Matt would sometimes take Sweetness out for a drive. One of these drives provided the opportunity for Payton to play one last prank on his friend: Sweetness said he wanted to visit their friend and teammate Mike Singletary. He gave Suhey directions to the house and Suhey went to the door, but it was not Singletary's place. An embarrassed Suhey had to apologize to the owners of the house, while Payton sat in the car laughing.

As his health declined, Payton did not go out much, because he was in pain and because he did not like people to see him in his weakened state. But he did like to make occasional trips to restaurants. He asked Suhey to take him on a tour of the top restaurants in Chicago. Payton had little appetite—he would order, at most, an appetizer—but he enjoyed the ambience of the restaurants.

Many people have noted that the relationship Payton and Suhey had was similar to the friendship between Bears legends Gale Sayers, who was black, and Brian Piccolo, who was white. As Piccolo was dying of cancer in 1970, his devoted friend Sayers was constantly at his side. Their story later formed the basis for the popular movie *Brian's Song*. However, Payton wryly noted, there was one big difference between that story and his own: "In that one, the white guy gets sick and dies. I said I wondered how come I couldn't be in that movie."

THE END

Late in October, Payton took a turn for the worse. His kidneys failed, and his body began to shut down. The end was clearly near. There was little anyone could do except make him as comfortable as possible. This was a difficult time for Connie, Jarrett, and Brittney, because their once strong husband and father had now become weak and dependent on their care. Connie commented:

> I think it was hard for the kids to see their dad getting sicker and more frail, but Walter was always smiling and staying positive. He was trying to be there for the kids, and he wanted them to know that their dad was there for them. Walter didn't want them to see him sick, because he knew in their eyes he was their Superman. . . .
>
> When he was ill and sleeping a lot, Walter spent time in each of the kids' rooms. . . . I don't know if he purposely spent time in their rooms to stay connected with them or if he just felt in his heart that he should be there. But after he died, Brittney and Jarrett said that they could feel his comforting presence in their rooms.

Connie made arrangements for Payton to spend his last days at their home in South Barrington. Jarrett came back from college. The rest of his family was there as well, including 14-year-old Brittney, who had just won a special award for courage from ESPN. Although Payton was in a lot of pain, he tried not to complain. His brother, Eddie, recalls,

Just a few weeks after his news conference, Walter Payton was diagnosed with cancer of the bile duct, which had spread to his lymph nodes. Eight months later, his kidneys failed, and he died shortly thereafter. Here, Jarrett Payton speaks to the media on November 1, 1999, to announce his father's death.

He knew what his fate was, never asked me why, never bitter, enjoyed every day that he was with us. He talked and laughed and joked with people who came in to visit as long . . . as his stamina would allow, and then he'd rest. Then he'd wake up and be ready to talk again. It was one of the most beautiful things that I'd ever witnessed and one of the greatest shows of courage that . . . I've ever witnessed.

Shortly after noon on November 1, 1999, Walter Payton died. His family was with him when he passed away. His sister, Pam Curry, later said, "To the very end, Walter lived like he played football . . . tough."

The news spread quickly. Bears offensive tackle Keith Van Horne was at home when he saw it on television. It was a shock to him—most of Sweetness's friends, like Van Horne, thought that he was still waiting for a transplant. "It tore a lot of people up and caught most people by surprise because we all thought he would pull through it. He was the last guy, I'm serious, he's the last guy on that team that anybody thought would leave us at such a young age. He had more energy than anybody."

"CHICAGO LOVED WALTER"

Two memorial services were held in the days after Payton's death. The first was a small, private ceremony at Life Changers International Church in Barrington, Illinois. Outside the church, 10 American flags flew at half-mast. Two others, one with the number 34 and one with the Bears logo, flew high above. Inside the church, the altar was covered with flowers. A color portrait of Payton in his Bears uniform and trademark white headband was prominently displayed. Payton's body had been cremated, and his ashes were in a vase on the altar.

This service was for family and close friends, although some Bears executives and public figures, including Chicago mayor Richard M. Daley and Illinois governor George Ryan, were also present. No media was allowed, although a few reporter friends were invited as guests.

The second service was a public memorial at Soldier Field on November 6. It was attended by an estimated 20,000 mourners who came to pay their last respects to the football great, including dozens of current and former Bears and NFL officials. Connie Payton was deeply moved by what she felt during this service: "Chicago loved Walter, and Walter loved Chicago. During that time on the field, everyone sensed that he wasn't far away." This public outpouring by Payton's fans affected Connie, Jarrett, and Brittney; it was easy to see how much Walter had touched the Chicago community. After Walter's death, Connie reflected on what the support of others meant to them:

> When my children and I look back on our last year with Walter, it wasn't just the support of family and friends that helped us get through the difficult times. We attribute a lot of that support to Walter's fans. For us, it's those fans that always believed in Walter, those who took the time to say a thank you when we needed it most. It's these special moments that we've held, and will continue to hold, dearest to our hearts.

REMEMBERING WALTER

During both the private and public memorials, a number of speakers reminisced about their friend, relative, and colleague. There was laughter as people remembered Payton's sunny attitude, fondness for jokes, and vibrant love of life. Bears trainer Clyde Emrich commented, "He was given ninety years, and he lived them all in forty-five."

There were also tears as people remembered how Payton's kindness and sweet nature helped him serve as a role model for others. Mike Ditka said, "He affected so many people in a positive way, not only through athletic prowess, but through his generosity and for the way he lived his life."

On November 6, 1999, the Chicago Bears held a memorial service for Walter Payton at Soldier Field. The service was attended by friends, family, former teammates, and nearly 20,000 fans. Here, members of the 1999 Bears place roses in front of a picture of Walter Payton during the tribute to the Hall of Famer.

And speakers reflected on Payton's amazing will to succeed. His brother, Eddie, said, "A lot of people ask me what motivated Walter to excel in everything he ever attempted. . . . I think of a great saying that [was] something that he lived by. . . . 'Each new day the good Lord gives me an opportunity to be good, better, or best. Each day I pledge to the Lord I will not rest until my good is better, and my better is the best.'"

And when Jarrett spoke, he reminisced about how he always heard his father's distinctive whistle—as a kid when he was playing in the yard, or as a young man when he was leaving the football field after a game. He said he could still hear it sometimes, and took comfort and encouragement from it.

Along with the stories, laughter, and tears that day, there also was a general feeling of relief that, in some ways, death was a blessing—that, at least, Payton was not in pain anymore. There also was a feeling that now was the time to reflect on the rich legacy that Sweetness had left behind.

Sweetness's Legacy

When he passed away, Walter Payton left behind a powerful and lasting legacy. As a result, he and his accomplishments will be remembered for many years to come.

Some of the ways in which Payton's memory lives on are physical and tangible. For example, a college prep high school in Chicago is named for him. At his alma mater, Jackson State University, students can walk down Walter Payton Place and work out in the 100,000-square-foot Walter Payton Recreation and Wellness Center. And two prominent awards are named in his honor: the Walter Payton Award, which is presented each year to the best offensive player in Division I-AA football, and the Walter Payton Man of the Year Award, which is given annually to an NFL player who not only excels on the field but also is devoted to charity and volunteer work in the community.

Walter Payton's brother, Eddie, presents the Walter Payton Award to Furman University tailback Louis Ivory in 2000. The award is presented annually to the top offensive football player in I-AA, the division Payton played in at Jackson State.

In Illinois, drivers can get a special license plate honoring Sweetness (the money goes toward supporting organ donations). And the Roundhouse restaurant, one of Payton's post-career business ventures, maintains a museum in his honor. It features such objects as the athlete's football and racing helmets, his Hall of Fame bust, some of his many awards, and scrapbooks with hundreds of articles.

A ROLE MODEL FOR OTHERS

Other aspects of Payton's legacy are less tangible. Perhaps the most important of these is the way in which generations of aspiring athletes have looked up to Payton as a role model.

Not that he ever thought of himself as someone to look up to; he once commented, "I'm not a role model. I'm just Walter Payton. . . . I'm human just like anybody else. I'm capable of making mistakes. . . . Nobody's perfect."

Nonetheless, countless athletes, both professional and amateur, have done just that—they have tried to be just like Payton. They have tried to emulate his physical toughness and grace, of course. But they have also tried to emulate something less easy to copy: his ability not to let being a celebrity get in the way of also being a good human being. Matt Suhey commented, "What Walter did better than any-one I've met was treat people right—everybody. There aren't many athletes out there today—especially superstars—who know how to do that."

One prominent example of an athlete who has tried to be like Payton is former Dallas Cowboys running back Emmitt Smith, who in 2002 broke the NFL career rushing record Payton had set back in 1984. After establishing the new record, Smith tearfully paid tribute to his childhood idol, saying that Sweetness had taught him how to conduct himself on and off the field. Payton's ability to give his all while remaining humble was what made him such a special person. He knew that success did not depend on money or fame. In his autobiography, Payton wrote:

> If you ask me how I want to be remembered, it is as a winner. Is a winner somebody who has success and basically accomplished something or wins a game or whatever? That's not a winner. You know what a win-ner is? A winner is somebody who has given his best effort, who has tried the hardest they possibly can, who has utilized every ounce of energy and strength within them to accomplish something. It doesn't mean they accomplished it or failed, it means that they've given it their best. . . . It doesn't mean that, Oh, God, I've got a lot of money, I've got a lot of success. . . .

I want to be remembered as a person who, whenever he played the game of football, he left everything he had out there on the football field, did everything he possibly could for the team to win, not for himself. For the team to win. [And] I want to be remembered as a guy who raised two pretty special kids and who taught them to be great people.

Today, players still admire Walter Payton. They watch tapes of his performance on the football field, continuing to marvel at and study his moves. Sometimes these amazing moves are not ones he was most famous for. Former Bears wide receiver Brian Baschnagel commented about one such move, "The most incredible thing I ever saw him do was the time he threw me a fifty-eight-yard touchdown pass. He was going down, two big linemen on him, and he not only had the strength to whip the ball that far sidearm, but also the presence of mind to realize he could do it."

Payton's legacy continues to have a deep, profound influence on today's NFL players. For example, Brett Favre stated:

Walter's mark on the NFL and football is just as great today as it was the day he retired. Right now there's a whole new generation of players coming up through the high schools and colleges down in Mississippi, like I did, and Walter Payton means as much to them as he does to me. He was just a phenomenal player and a phenomenal person who overcame the odds to succeed. He always represented the very best as a player and as a person. And that's why his legacy lives on today.

In addition, Payton has been a lasting inspiration to football fans both young and old. One fan, Tom Borst, lived near the Payton family. He recalled how he once saw the athlete working out. Payton was running up and down a hill on a day of miserable weather, six months before the start of training camp.

That sight, Borst says, has given him inspiration countless times in the years since. He commented, "I'm sure there's many other things Walter Payton could have done that cold, rainy day. I can't tell you how many times I haven't felt like doing something and I think back to that day—what a glorious vision Walter Payton was that miserable day."

PHILANTHROPY

Walter Payton's legacy and spirit live on in other ways as well, such as the charitable foundation he started. During his life, Payton always put a strong emphasis on philanthropy—that is, doing good works and giving to charity. He tried hard to give something back to society, because he felt he had received so much from people throughout the years.

He once commented that this feeling had been ingrained in him since childhood: "My understanding of the obligations of fame and wealth comes from my father. He told me when I was young that it was your responsibility, once you've had some success, to reach back and bring someone with you."

Consequently, he established the Walter Payton Foundation in 1989. (The name was later changed to the Walter and Connie Payton Foundation.) The athlete saw this organization as a way to give something to the community that had been so good to him. (It was originally called the George Halas/Walter Payton Foundation and run jointly with the family of George Halas, who owned the Bears when Payton joined the team. The name was changed in 1998.)

WISHES TO SANTA

Sweetness's foundation was, and is, involved with several charitable endeavors. Its main focus is to provide financial support and motivation for young but disadvantaged people, helping them raise the quality of life for themselves and those around them. To

MORE THAN JUST A GUY ON A MOTORCYCLE

Many of Walter Payton's friends and former teammates have their own stories about his ability to light up a room. After all, his smile was contagious, and he made everyone feel important. Payton's impact on others is illustrated well by one of the players who blocked for him on the football field. Chicago Bears center/guard Tom Thayer played with Walter Payton for three seasons—from 1985 to 1987—but he grew up in the suburbs of Chicago and thus idolized the Bears' Hall of Fame running back from an early age. Today, Thayer is the color commentator for Bears broadcasts on the Chicago radio station WBBM. In the following passage, Thayer recounted how Payton went out of his way to treat people well and bring a smile to their faces:

> I come from a close family in Joliet [just outside Chicago], and every Sunday afternoon my mom cooks a big meal and all my nieces and nephews and brothers and sisters come over. One Sunday afternoon Walter shows up on his motorcycle, and he sat there with my family, and kids from the neighborhood were coming over, and they sat on his lap and sat on the motorcycle, and we had so much fun that day.
>
> The smile on his face is what I'll always remember, and these little kids didn't know at the time that here was one of the greatest football players in history. They just saw this guy showing up on his motorcycle, and they were laughing and giggling. That day was pretty awesome to me, the fact that he would take that time to show up and present himself like that.

this end, it organizes such programs as a Back to School Supply Drive and charity auctions of sports memorabilia.

But the foundation's best-known program is the Holiday Giving Program. The program collects Christmas gifts for abused and neglected children in Illinois. It has been very successful, annually providing tens of thousands of kids with gift bags of new, high-quality toys and clothes.

To Payton, the creation of the Holiday Giving Program was a major achievement. Receiving Christmas gifts, he felt, goes a long way toward helping "forgotten" kids in the social service system, by giving them a measure of self-esteem. He commented, "Gifts on Christmas for abused and neglected children may not seem like a lot, but in terms of establishing self-worth, confidence, and a feeling of pride, I believe it may mean everything."

THE FAMILY CONTINUES

The Payton family has continued to honor Walter's legacy in several ways. One important way has been recognizing the importance of service to others. Connie Payton commented, "Walter made me realize that your own life can get pretty boring, but if you live life outside of yourself, and think about what you can do for other people and what you can do to make a difference, I mean, honestly, you wake up every morning feeling good about yourself."

Jarrett Payton has followed in his father's footsteps in more than one way. Jarrett, like his father, played running back in college and in the NFL. Jarrett signed with the Tennessee Titans as an undrafted rookie free agent out of the University of Miami in 2004. Although he did not see any action with the Titans that season, he played in NFL Europe with the Amsterdam Admirals and helped them win World Bowl XIII in the spring

Walter Payton's wife, Connie, is involved in many philanthropic endeavors, including promoting organ and tissue donation. Here, she speaks during an October 2000 news conference raising awareness for this cause. Joining Payton are, from left to right: Illinois senator Dick Durbin, former Washington Redskins kicker Mark Moseley and defensive end Bill Brundige, Pinnacle Management Group president and CEO George Beim, Ohio senator Mike DeWine, Tennessee Titans marketing director Ralph Ockenfels, and Michigan senator Carl Levin. To Payton's left is 5-year-old heart transplant recipient John Hochstein.

of 2005. That fall, he rushed for 105 yards on 33 carries and scored two touchdowns for the Titans. He was then released by the team prior to the 2006 season. In 2007, he signed a one-year contract with the Montreal Alouettes of the Canadian Football League. Jarrett also frequently speaks in public on behalf of the Walter Payton Foundation. He commented, "My father's legacy isn't all that complicated: Be the very best you can be, and the rest will follow. Don't focus on what you can't control, but only on what you can. Just do your best by giving everything you've got and leaving it all out on the field."

Jarrett adds that people often ask him what it was like growing up as the son of a superstar. He points out that in the 1980s his father was to Chicago what Michael Jordan was to that city in the 1990s. He said, "But despite all the fame, I always loved my dad for being so down to earth, for knowing that at the end of the day, it was the love he shared with me, my mom and my sister that mattered most."

Meanwhile, Brittney has followed her father's example in her devotion to community service. After her father became ill, while she was still in high school, Brittney cofounded Youth For Life, a network of students who help educate teens nationwide about the need for organ donation. The group sponsors activities such as programs encouraging teens to register as organ donors when they get their driver's license. Youth For Life has remained a major focus of Brittney's life, even after she has gone on to become a student at DePaul University in Chicago.

Payton's wife and children continue to feel Sweetness's presence in many ways. Connie Payton remarked that this is especially true with the memories they have of him. "These are the things that we hold on to," she said. "When I look at the picture from the night of Brittney's eighth-grade dance, there is a sweetness and a sadness to it. You can see how proud of her he looks and how happy she is to have him there."

Jarrett and Brittney collaborated in 2005 with their mother to write a book, *Payton*, about their famous father and husband. They also still help oversee the philanthropic work of the Walter Payton Foundation. Connie Payton also oversees her own foundation, which focuses on raising money for cancer research, and is involved in other projects, such as State Farm Insurance's "Embrace Life Awards," which honors women who have survived the loss of a spouse. She stated:

During his life, Walter Payton touched a number of people, and his legacy goes well beyond his accomplishments on the football field. He will forever be known as "Sweetness," a man whose sunny disposition could bring a smile to anyone's face.

Life is short and yet it's good, and there's so much to do. It's just a privilege for me to be able to continue Walter's legacy. . . . It was who he was and what he was about, touching lives and opening up to people and making them feel welcome and giving them some hope and just being warm.

By remaining involved in community service, each of the surviving Paytons can maintain a little bit of the close connection they had with Sweetness when he was alive. Jarrett commented, "Every day I start to understand my dad a lot more.

What kind of warrior he was. How he fought. I'm proud to be Walter's son." Brittney added, "I wear his Super Bowl ring every day. My mom gave it to me a few years ago and that's something that's very special to me." And Connie Payton reflected,

> I have to pinch myself sometimes because it [Payton's death] still feels like it's not real. I still feel his presence so closely. There's not a day that goes by when I don't meet somebody and they tell me a story about Walter and how he touched them in some small way. It's unbelievable sometimes how much love and admiration people still feel for Walter and how they still talk about him as if he's still here and playing today.

STATISTICS

WALTER PAYTON
POSITION: Running back

FULL NAME:
Walter Jerry Payton
BORN: July 25, 1954,
Columbia, Mississippi
HEIGHT: 5'10"
WEIGHT: 200 lbs.

COLLEGE:
Jackson State
University
TEAM:
Chicago Bears
(1975–1987)

YEAR	TEAM	G	ATT	YDS	Y/C	TD	REC	YDS	Y/R	TC
1975	CHI	13	196	679	3.5	7	33	213	6.5	0
1976	CHI	14	311	1,390	4.5	13	15	149	9.9	0
1977	CHI	14	339	1,852	5.5	14	27	269	10.0	2
1978	CHI	16	333	1,395	4.2	11	50	480	9.6	0
1979	CHI	16	369	1,610	4.4	14	31	313	10.1	2
1980	CHI	16	317	1,460	4.6	6	46	367	8.0	1
1981	CHI	16	339	1,222	3.6	6	41	379	9.2	2
1982	CHI	9	148	596	4.0	1	32	311	9.7	0
1983	CHI	16	314	1,421	4.5	6	53	607	11.5	2
1984	CHI	16	381	1,684	4.4	11	45	368	8.2	0
1985	CHI	16	324	1,551	4.8	9	49	483	9.9	2
1986	CHI	16	321	1,333	4.2	8	37	382	10.3	3
1987	CHI	12	146	533	3.7	4	33	217	6.6	1
TOTALS		190	3,838	16,726	4.4	110	492	4,538	9.2	15

CHRONOLOGY

1954	**July 25** Walter Payton is born in Columbia, Mississippi.
1967–1971	Plays sports, including football, for Jefferson High School and Columbia High School.
1971	Joins older brother, Eddie, on the football team at Jackson State University.
1974	Graduates from Jackson State with a bachelor's degree in communications; wraps up his football career by being named Little All-American after scoring 66 touchdowns and rushing for 3,563 yards.
1975	**January 28** Selected in the first round of the NFL draft by the Chicago Bears, as the fourth pick overall. **November 16** Rushes for 105 yards on 23 carries in a 31-3 loss at San Francisco—it is the first 100-yard game of his NFL career.
1976	Marries his college sweetheart, Connie Norwood; records his first 1,000-yard season: 311 rushing attempts for 1,390 yards; selected to the Pro Bowl, the first of nine times.
1977	Has his first 200-yard game (23 carries for 205 yards, in a 26-0 win at Green Bay on October 30); sets the NFL single-game rushing record (275 yards) in a 10-7 win over Minnesota on November 20; wins the first of two league MVP awards.
1984	Breaks former Cleveland running back Jim Brown's NFL all-time career rushing mark of 12,312 yards in a 20-7 win over the New Orleans Saints on October 7; also breaks Brown's record of 58 100-yard rushing games.
1985	Wins his second NFL MVP Award.
1986	**January 26** The Bears win the most lopsided contest in Super Bowl history, defeating the New England Patriots,

46-10, in Super Bowl XX; Payton rushes for 61 yards on 22 carries in the game and does not score a touchdown.

1987   Joins board of directors for the Chicago Bears; Walter Payton Award, honoring the nation's top offensive player in Division I-AA, established.
December 20 Plays his final regular-season game at Soldier Field against Seattle, a 34-21 loss.

1988   **January 10** Retires at the age of 33 after 21-17 loss to the Washington Redskins in the divisional round of the NFC playoffs; ends his career having played in 186 consecutive games; becomes executive director of

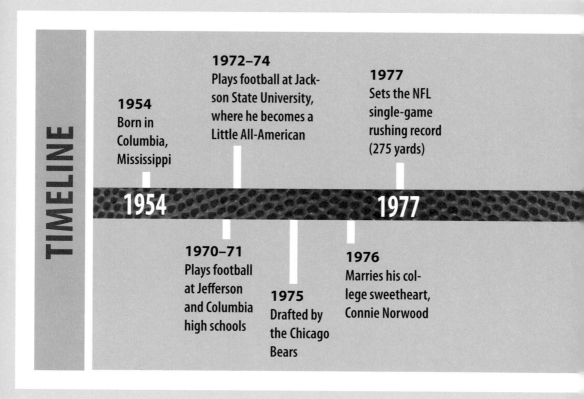

TIMELINE

1954
Born in Columbia, Mississippi

1972–74
Plays football at Jackson State University, where he becomes a Little All-American

1977
Sets the NFL single-game rushing record (275 yards)

1954   **1977**

1970–71
Plays football at Jefferson and Columbia high schools

1975
Drafted by the Chicago Bears

1976
Marries his college sweetheart, Connie Norwood

George Halas/Walter Payton Foundation benefiting neglected and abused children.

1992   Makes his debut as professional race car driver.

1993   July 31 Inducted into the Pro Football Hall of Fame during his first year of eligibility; his son, Jarrett, introduces him at the induction ceremony in Canton, Ohio.

1994   Named to NFL's 75th Anniversary Team.

1995   Becomes co-owner of Payton/Coyne Racing, an Indy-car team.

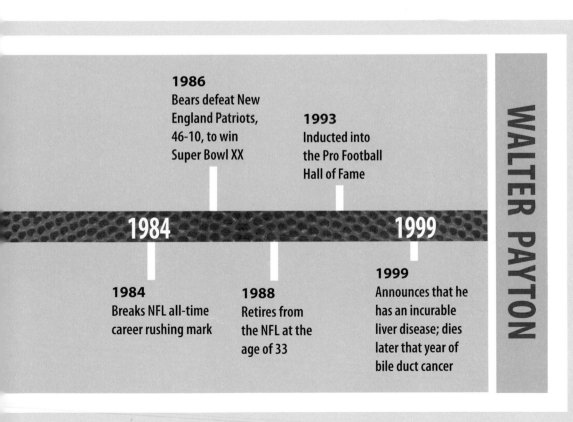

1986
Bears defeat New England Patriots, 46-10, to win Super Bowl XX

1993
Inducted into the Pro Football Hall of Fame

1984

1999

1984
Breaks NFL all-time career rushing mark

1988
Retires from the NFL at the age of 33

1999
Announces that he has an incurable liver disease; dies later that year of bile duct cancer

WALTER PAYTON

1996   Inducted into the College Football Hall of Fame in South Bend, Indiana; Walter Payton's Roundhouse complex opens in Aurora, Illinois.

1999   **February 2** Announces publicly that he has an incurable liver disease, primary sclerosing cholangitis (PSC), and is seeking a transplant.
November 1 Dies of bile duct cancer at home at the age of 45 with his wife, Connie; son, Jarrett; and daughter, Brittney at his side; voted number 39 among North American athletes of the twentieth century by ESPN's SportsCentury panel.

GLOSSARY

American Football Conference (AFC)   One of the two conferences in the National Football League (NFL). The AFC was established after the NFL merged with the American Football League (AFL) in 1970.

audible   A play called by the quarterback at the line of scrimmage to change the play called in the huddle.

backup   A second-string player who does not start the game, but comes in later in relief of a starter.

blitz   A defensive maneuver in which one or more linebackers or defensive backs, who normally remain behind the line of scrimmage, instead charge into the opponent's backfield.

blocking   When a player obstructs another player's path with his body. Examples: cut block, zone block, trap block, pull block, screen block, pass block, and double-team block.

bootleg   An offensive play predicated upon misdirection in which the quarterback pretends to hand the ball to another player and then carries the ball in the opposite direction of the supposed ballcarrier with the intent of either passing or running (sometimes the quarterback has the option of doing either).

center   A player position on offense. The center snaps the ball.

chain   The 10-yard-long chain that is used by the chain crew (aka, "chain gang") to measure for a new series of downs.

completion percentage   The percentage of passes thrown by a player that are completed. For example, if a running back throws one pass all season and completes it, his completion percentage would be 100 percent.

cornerback   A defensive back who lines up near the line of scrimmage across from a wide receiver. His primary job is to disrupt passing routes and to defend against short and medium passes in the passing game and to contain the rusher on running plays.

defensive back   A cornerback or safety position on the defensive team; commonly defends against wide receivers on passing plays. Generally there are four defensive backs playing at a time.

defensive end   A player position on defense who lines up on the outside of the defensive line whose principal function is to deliver pressure to the quarterback.

defensive tackle   A player position on defense on the inside of the defensive line whose principal function is to contain the run.

drive   A continuous set of offensive plays gaining substantial yardage and several first downs, usually leading to a scoring opportunity.

end zone   The area between the end line and the goal line, bounded by the sidelines.

extra point   A single point scored in a conversion attempt after a touchdown by place- or drop-kicking the ball through the opponent's goal.

field goal   Score of three points made by place- or drop-kicking the ball through the opponent's goal.

first down   The first of a set of four downs. Usually, a team that has a first down needs to advance the ball 10 yards to receive another first down, but penalties or field position (i.e., less than 10 yards from the opposing end zone) can affect this.

formation   An arrangement of the offensive skill players.

fourth down   The final of a set of four downs. Unless a first down is achieved or a penalty forces a replay of the down, the team will lose control of the ball after this play. If a team does not think they can get a first down, they often punt on fourth down or kick a field goal if they are close enough to do so.

fullback   A player position on offense. In modern formations, this position may be varied, and this player has more
blocking responsibilities in comparison to the halfback or
tailback.

fumble   A ball that a player accidentally loses possession of.

goal line   The front of the end zone.

guard   One of two player positions on offense (linemen).

handoff   A player's handing of a live ball to another player.
The handoff goes either backwards or laterally, as opposed
to a forward pass.

holding   There are two kinds of holding: offensive holding, illegally blocking a player from the opposing team by
grabbing and holding his uniform or body; and defensive
holding, called against defensive players who impede
receivers who are more than five yards from the line of
scrimmage, but who are not actively making an attempt to
catch the ball.

huddle   An on-field gathering of members of a team in order
to secretly communicate instructions for the upcoming play.

incomplete pass   A forward pass of the ball that no player
legally caught.

interception   The legal catching of a forward pass thrown by
an opposing player.

kickoff   A free kick that starts each half, or restarts the game
following a touchdown or field goal.

line of scrimmage/scrimmage line   One of two vertical planes
parallel to the goal line when the ball is to be put in play by
scrimmage.

linebacker   A player position on defense. The linebackers
typically play one to six yards behind the defensive linemen
and are the most versatile players on the field because they
can play both run and pass defense or are called to blitz.

man-to-man coverage   A defense in which all players in pass coverage, typically linebackers and defensive backs, cover a specific player.

National Collegiate Athletic Association (NCAA)   Principal governing body of college sports, including college football.

National Football Conference (NFC)   One of the two conferences in the National Football League (NFL). The NFC was established after the NFL merged with the American Football League (AFL) in 1970.

National Football League (NFL)   The largest professional American football league, with 32 teams.

offside   An infraction of the rule that requires both teams to be on their own side of their restraining line as or before the ball is put in play. Offside is typically called on the defensive team.

option   A type of play in which the quarterback has the option of handing off, keeping, or laterally passing to one or more backs. Often described by a type of formation or play action, such as triple option, veer option, or counter option.

pass interference   When a player illegally hinders an eligible receiver's opportunity to catch a forward pass.

passer rating   (also **quarterback rating**) A numeric value used to measure the performance of quarterbacks. It was formulated in 1973 and it uses the player's completion percentage, passing yards, touchdowns, and interceptions.

play action   A tactic in which the quarterback fakes either a handoff or a throw in order to draw the defense away from the intended offensive method.

pocket   An area on the offensive side of the line of scrimmage, where the offensive linemen attempt to prevent the defensive players from reaching the quarterback during passing plays.

position   A place where a player plays relative to teammates, and/or a role filled by that player.

punt   A kick in which the ball is dropped and kicked before it reaches the ground. Used to give up the ball to the opposition after offensive downs have been used.

quarterback   An offensive player who lines up behind the center, from whom he takes the snap.

reception   When a player catches (receives) the ball.

running back   A player position on offense. Although the term usually refers to the halfback or tailback, fullbacks are also considered running backs.

sack   Tackling a ballcarrier who intends to throw a forward pass. A sack also is awarded if a player forces a fumble of the ball, or the ballcarrier to go out of bounds, behind the line of scrimmage on an apparent intended forward pass play.

safety   A player position on defense; a method of scoring (worth two points) by downing an opposing ballcarrier in his own end zone, forcing the opposing ballcarrier out of his own end zone and out of bounds, or forcing the offensive team to fumble the ball so that it exits the end zone.

salary cap   A limit on the amount any NFL team can spend on its players' salaries; the salary cap was introduced in 1994 in order to bring parity to the NFL.

scramble   On a called passing play, when the quarterback runs from the pocket in an attempt to avoid being sacked, giving the receivers more time to get open or attempting to gain positive yards by running himself.

secondary   Refers to the defensive "backfield," specifically the safeties and cornerbacks.

shotgun formation   Formation in which offensive team may line up at the start of a play. In this formation, the quarterback receives the snap five to eight yards behind the center.

sideline   One of the lines marking each side of the field.

snap   The handoff or pass from the center that begins a play from scrimmage.

special teams   The units that handle kickoffs, punts, free kicks, and field-goal attempts.

starter   A player who is the first to play his position within a given game or season. Depending on the position and the game situation, this player may be replaced or share time with one or more players later in the game. For example, a quarterback may start the game but be replaced by a backup quarterback if the game becomes one-sided.

tackle   The act of forcing a ballcarrier to the ground. Also, a position on the offensive and defensive line.

tailback   Player position on offense farthest ("deepest") back, except in kicking formations.

tight end   A player position on offense, often known as a Y receiver, when he lines up on the line of scrimmage next to the offensive tackle. Tight ends are used as blockers during running plays and either run a route or stay in to block during passing plays.

time of possession   The amount of time one team has the ball in its possession relative to the other team.

touchdown   A play worth six points, accomplished by gaining legal possession of the ball in the opponent's end zone. It also allows the team a chance for one extra point by kicking the ball or a chance to convert a two-point conversion.

turnover   The loss of the ball by one team to the other team. This is usually the result of a fumble or an interception.

West Coast offense   An offensive philosophy that uses short, high-percentage passes as the core of a ball-control offense.

wide receiver   A player position on offense. He is split wide (usually about 10 yards) from the formation and plays on the line of scrimmage as a split end (X) or one yard off as a flanker (Z).

wild card   The two playoff spots given to the two nondivision winning teams that have the best records in each conference.

wishbone   A formation involving three running backs lined up behind the quarterback in the shape of a Y, similar to the shape of a wishbone.

yard   One yard of linear distance in the direction of one of the two goals. A field is 100 yards. Typically, a team is required to advance at least 10 yards in order to get a new set of downs.

zone defense   A defense in which players who are in pass coverage cover zones of the field, instead of individual players.

BIBLIOGRAPHY

Payton, Connie, Jarrett, and Brittney. *Payton*. New York: Rugged Land, 2005.

Payton, Walter, with Don Yaeger. *Never Die Easy: The Autobiography of Walter Payton*. New York: Villard, 2000.

Towle, Mike. *I Remember Walter Payton*. Nashville, Tenn.: Cumberland House, 2000.

FURTHER READING

Fantle, Tom, and Tom Johnson. *Sweetness: The Courage and Heart of Walter Payton*. Chicago, Ill.: Triumph Books, 1999.

Italia, Bob. *The Chicago Bears*. Edina, Minn.: Abdo and Daughters, 1996.

Smith, Ron. *Heroes of the Hall: Pro Football's Greatest Players*. St. Louis, Mo.: The Sporting News, 2003.

Towle, Mike. *Walter Payton: Football's "Sweetest" Superstar*. Nashville, Tenn.: Cumberland House, 2005.

WEB SITES

Chicago Bears Tribute to Walter Payton
http://www.bearshistory.com/lore/walterpayton.aspx

Tribute to Walter Payton
http://www.dailyherald.com/special/payton/stories.html

The Walter and Connie Payton Foundation
http://www.payton34.com

Walter Payton Cancer Fund
http://www.payton34.org/

Pro Football Hall of Fame: Walter Payton
http://www.profootballhof.com/hof/member.jsp?player_id=174

Sporting News: Walter Payton
http://www.sportingnews.com/archives/payton/

United Network for Organ Sharing: Organ Donation and Transplantation
http://www.unos.org/

DVD

Chicago Bears—The Complete History. Warner Home Video, 2005. This two-disc set includes plenty on Walter Payton and the NFL Films production of Super Bowl XX, Payton's and the Bears' triumphant win against the Patriots.

PICTURE CREDITS

INDEX

A

AIDS rumor, 91–92
Alcorn State University, 27, 37
Amsterdam Admirals, 109
Anderson, Neal, 76
aneurysms, 61
Anheuser-Busch, 85
Arizona Cardinals, 67, 83
Armstrong, Neill, 10, 61
Atlanta Falcons, 39
auto racing, 86–88
automobile accident, 88

B

Back to School Supply Drives, 109
Baker, Douglas, 34, 35
balance, 23
Baltimore Colts, 39, 44, 56
Banks, Ernie, 13
Barbour, Haley, 18
Barrington, Illinois, 99
Bartkowski, Steve, 39
Baschnagel, Brian, 106
Bears. *See* Chicago Bears
Beim, George, 110
Bell, Todd, 66
bile ducts, cancer of, 94
Black College offensive player of the year award, 37
Board of Education, Brown v., 21–22
Borst, Tom, 106–107
Boston, Charles, 24
brain aneurysm, 61
Brazile, Robert, 7, 30
Brekke, Dan, 60
Breland, Quin, 23–24
Brewer, Jill, 25
Brian's Song, 96–97
Bridgestone/Firestone Tires, 81
Brown, Jim, breaking rushing record of, 11, 64, 65, 67

Brown v. Board of Education, 21–22
Brundige, Bill, 110
Bryant, Paul "Bear," 26
Buffalo Bills, 51
Buffone, Doug, 44
Burke, Cheryl, 33

C

Canadian Football League, 110
cancer of bile ducts, 94
Canton, Ohio, 86
cars, love of, 87–88
Casem, Marino, 37
CBS This Morning, 94
charities, 10, 15, 107–113
Charlotte, North Carolina, 84
Cherry, Deron, 84
Chicago, adjusting to life in, 42–44
Chicago Bears
   career with, 9–11
   closeness with after retirement, 81
   fans of, 12–13
   memorial service of, 100–102
   playoffs and, 67–68
   signing with, 39–40
   Super Bowl XX and, 70–74
Chicago Bulls, 12, 13
Chicago Cubs, 13, 65
cholangitis, primary sclerosing
   death from, 15, 97–98
   diagnosis and, 90–91
   early signs of, 89–90
   fighting, 92–96
   Matt Suhey and, 96–97
   memorials and, 100–102
   public announcement of, 91–92
Christmas charities, 109
Cincinnati Bengals, 52
Cleveland Browns, 11, 28, 29, 64
Clinton, Jerry, 85

coaching, lack of interest in,
    81–82
college football
    Eddie Payton and, 21
    life during, 35–38
    memorials to Payton and, 103
    playing of, 27–31
Columbia, Mississippi, childhood
    in, 16–17
Columbia High School, 22–25

D
Daley, Richard M., 99
Dallas Cowboys, 33, 39, 62, 66
dancing, 32, 33
Dancing with the Stars, 33
Daniels, L. E., 25
Dantin, Forrest, 22
Davis, Anthony, 36
Davis, Tommy, 24
death of Walter Payton, 97–99
Dent, Richard, 68
DePaul University, 111
depression, 85–86
Detroit Lions, 28, 67
DeWine, Mike, 110
Dillon, Corey, 52, 53
Ditka, Mike
    on Payton breaking Brown's
        rushing record, 67
    improvement of Bears and,
        10–11, 61–63
    on Payton as role model, 100
    on skill of Payton, 9
    Super Bowl XX and, 70
    training regimen of Payton, 14
divorce, filing for, 86
drafts, 39
drug abuse rumor, 91–92
Durbin, Dick, 110

E
education. *See also* Jackson State
    University

academic success and, 25
focus on, 17, 34–35
integration and, 21–23
Jefferson High School and,
    20–21
Elkhart Lake, Wisconsin, 88
"Embrace Life Awards,"
    111–112
Emrich, Clyde, 100
ESPN, 97
expansion teams, 83–84, 85

F
fans
    answering letters from, 81
    illness and, 95
    inspiration to, 106–107
    memorials and, 100
    Payton's appreciation of,
        12–13
    popularity with, 58–60
Favre, Brett, 54–55, 106
Fencik, Gary, 68
Finks, Jim, 42, 86
firecrackers, 56
Flores, Tom, 70
friendships, 57–58
Furman University, 104

G
Gamauf, John, 81
Gandhi, Mahatma, 91
gardens, 17
Gault, Willie, 54, 63, 68, 72
George Halas/Walter Payton
    Foundation, 107
Giangreco, Mark, 91
Gibron, Abe, 42
goal-line leap, 48–49
Graves, Ricky Joe, 22
Green Bay Packers, 46, 54, 55
Grambling State University,
    37
Griffin, Archie, 36

H

Halas, George, 107
Hall of Fame, 86, 87
Hampton, Dan, 63, 68
Harper, Roland
    on adjusting to Chicago, 43
    friendship with, 57–58
    on sense of humor, 56
Harris, Franco, 64–65, 67
Heisman Trophy, 36–37
Hill, Bob, 10, 30, 31–32
Hochstein, John, 110
Holiday Giving Program, 109
Holmes, Bud, 76
Huff, Ken, 39
humor
    childhood and, 19
    college life and, 35
    during illness, 96
    love of, 14–15
    teammates and, 55–57
    use of to break tension,
        22
hunting, 60–61

I

illness
    death from, 15, 97–98
    diagnosis and, 90–91
    early signs of, 89–90
    fighting, 92–96
    Matt Suhey and, 96–97
    memorials and, 100–102
    public announcement of,
        91–92
injuries, 13, 45, 75–76
integration, 21–23
investments, 82–83, 84–86
Ivory, Louis, 104

J

Jackson (Mississippi) *Clarion-
    Ledger*, 33

Jackson State University
    Eddie Payton and, 21
    life at, 35–38
    memorials to Payton at, 103
    playing for, 27–31
Jacksonville, Florida, 84
Jaycettes, 33
Jefferson High School, 20–21,
    22–23
Jiggetts, Dan, 82
Johnson, Gary, 37
jokes
    childhood and, 19
    college life and, 35
    during illness, 96
    love of, 14–15
    teammates and, 55–57
    use of to break tension, 22
Jordan, Michael, 13, 111

K

Kansas, University of, 27
Kansas City Chiefs, 28, 84
Kemp, Jack, 18

L

Lambeau Field, 14
Lamborghini, 65–66
Larry King Live, 94
lawsuits, 84–86
leadership, 54–55
Levin, Carl, 110
Lewis, Jamal, 53
license plates, 104
Life Changers International
    Church, 99–100
Little All-American, 36
liver disease. *See* primary scleros-
    ing cholangitis (PSC)
long jump, 25
Los Angeles Memorial Coliseum,
    8
Los Angeles Raiders, 70
Los Angeles Rams, 70, 71, 84

M

Madden, John, 15
Magrane, Bill, 42–43, 44, 72
Man of the Year Award, 103
Marshall, Wilbur, 68
Mayo Clinic, 90
McCarren, Larry, 46–47
McFadden Ventures, 83
McMahon, Jim, 63, 68–70, 72, 74
McMichael, Steve, 68
memorial services, 99–102
Memphis, Tennessee, 28
Metalious, Grace, 28
Miami Dolphins, 45, 70
Minnesota Vikings, 51–52
Mississippi Maniac, 87
money, investing, 82–83
Montreal Alouettes, 110
Moses, Edward, 21, 24
Moseley, Mark, 110
motivational speaking, 81–82
motorcycle story, 108

N

National Basketball Association
   (NBA), 12
New England Patriots, 70–74
New Orleans, Louisiana, 32, 70
New Orleans Saints, 49, 65, 66
New York Giants, 70
Newman, Paul, 88
NFL Europe, 109
NFL MVP Award, 12, 51
NFL team ownership, 83–84
nicknames, 7
Norwood, Connie (wife). See
   Payton, Connie (wife)
number 34, retiring of, 78–79

O

Oakland Raiders, 15, 83
Ockenfels, Ralph, 110
Ohio State University, 36

Oprah Winfrey Show, The, 94
organ donation, 91, 94–96, 111

P

Pardee, Jack, 10, 13, 42, 45
Patriots, 70–74
Payton (Payton family), 111
Payton, Alyne (mother), 16–18,
   43–44
Payton, Brittney (daughter)
   auto racing crash and, 88
   public service and, 111, 113
   retirement and, 15
   on sense of humor, 74
Payton, Connie (wife)
   anniversary and, 74–75
   dating, 32–34
   death of Payton and, 97–100
   divorce petition and, 86
   early time in Chicago and, 44
   on fun, 69–70
   initial meeting with, 31–32
   legacy of Payton and, 111–112
   life with, 60–61
   marriage to, 50
   on public service, 109–110
   retirement and, 15
Payton, Eddie (brother)
   childhood with, 16
   football career of, 20–21
   on illness and death of Payton,
      97–99
   Jackson State University and,
      28–29
   work ethic of Payton family
      and, 17, 18
Payton, Jarrett (son)
   birth of, 61
   death announcement and,
      98–99
   football career of, 109–111
   Hall of Fame induction speech
      and, 86, 87
   Lamborghini and, 66

legacy of Payton and, 110–113
memorial service and, 101
press conference of, 91
retirement and, 15
Payton, Pam (sister), 16, 17, 18, 99
Payton, Peter (father), 16–17, 61
Payton Award, 103–104
Payton Foundation, 10, 107, 110, 111
Payton Man of the Year Award, 103
Payton Power Equipment, 83
Payton Recreation and Wellness Center, 103
Payton's Place, 28–29
Payton's Roundhouse, 83
Pearl River, 19
Perry, Vernon, 34–35
Perry, William, 68
Peterson, Adrian, 53
Peyton Place, 28–29
Philadelphia Eagles, 62
philanthropy, 10, 15, 107–113
Phillips, Rodney, 34, 35
Phoenix, Arizona, 83, 85
Piccolo, Brian, 96–97
Pierson, Don, 57
Pioneer Recovery Systems, 17
poverty, 16
practical jokes
    childhood and, 19
    college life and, 35
    during illness, 96
    love of, 14–15
    teammates and, 55–57
    use of to break tension, 22
primary sclerosing cholangitis (PSC)
    death from, 15, 97–98
    diagnosis and, 90–91
    early signs of, 89–90
    fighting, 92–96
    Matt Suhey and, 96–97

memorials and, 100–102
public announcement of, 91–92
Pro Football Hall of Fame, 86, 87
public service, 10, 15, 107–113

R
racing, 86–88
radio shows, 80–81
Reagan, Ronald, 65
restaurants, 83, 104
retirement. *See also* public service
    illness and, 15
    last game and, 78–79
    reluctance and, 76–77
    statistics at, 11–12
role model, legacy as, 104–107
Rosemont, Illinois, 92, 93
Roundhouse, Walter Payton's, 83, 104
running style, 46, 47
rushing yards records, 53, 64, 67
Ryan, George, 99

S
San Diego Padres, 65
San Francisco 49ers, 59, 68, 70
Sanders, Barry, 67
Sanders, Deion, 57
Sayers, Gale
    Brian Piccolo and, 96–97
    Chicago Bears and, 40, 41, 50
scholarships, 25–27
sclerosing cholangitis
    death from, 15, 97–98
    diagnosis and, 90–91
    early signs of, 89–90
    fighting, 92–96
    Matt Suhey and, 96–97
    memorials and, 100–102
    public announcement of, 91–92
Seattle Seahawks, 47, 64, 78, 79

segregation, 16, 21–23
shoelaces, untying of, 15
Shreveport, Louisiana, 43
Simpson, O. J., 51
Singletary, Mike, 63, 68, 96
Smith, Emmitt
    Dancing with the Stars and, 33
    Payton as idol of, 105
    rushing yards records and, 66
Smith Quarter neighborhood, 16
Soldier Field, 100, 101
Soul Train, 32, 33
South Barrington, Illinois, 97
Southwestern Athletic Conference (SWAC), 35
Sporting News, 91
sports shows, 80–81
St. Louis Cardinals, 83, 85
St. Louis, Missouri, expansion team project, 83–84
St. Louis Sun, 83
strikes, 52–53
stutter step, 54
Suhey, Matt
    diagnosis of Payton and, 90–91
    friendship with, 58, 59, 96–97
    on leadership, 69
    on sense of humor, 56
    on taking a beating, 76
"Super Bowl Shuffle," 69–70
Super Bowl XX, 70–74

T
Tagliabue, Paul, 11
Tampa Bay Buccaneers, 69
Telander, Rick, 65
Tennessee Titans, 109–110
Thayer, Tom, 108
Tobin, Bill, 40
topsoil chore, 17–18
touchdown in wrong end zone, 23
Touched by an Angel, 94
Towle, Mike, 42

training regimen
    benefits of, 46
    difficulty of, 13–14, 31
    weight training and, 24–25
transplants, 91, 94–96, 111
Tucker, Kim, 81
24 Karat Black Gold, 32

U
University of Alabama, 26
University of Florida, 76
University of Kansas, 27
University of Miami, 91, 109
University of Southern California, 36
University of Southern Mississippi, 26
U.S. Marines, 14
USA Football, 18

V
Van Horne, Keith, 56, 99
video, 69–70

W
Walter Payton Award, 103–104
Walter Payton Foundation, 10, 107, 110, 111
Walter Payton Man of the Year Award, 103
Walter Payton Power Equipment, 83
Walter Payton Recreation and Wellness Center, 103
Walter Payton's Roundhouse, 83, 104
war game, 20
Washington Redskins, 68, 74, 79
weight training, 24
White, Randy, 39
World Bowl XIII, 109

Y
Youth for Life, 111

ABOUT THE AUTHOR

ADAM WOOG has written more than 60 books for adults, young adults, and children. He has special interests in music, biography, and history. Woog holds a master's degree in communications from Antioch University. He lives with his family in his hometown of Seattle, Washington, where he cheers for his daughter Leah's high school varsity basketball squad.